THE LANDSCAPING REVOLUTION

Garden with Mother Nature, Not Against Her

ANDY WASOWSKI with SALLY WASOWSKI

Photographs by Andy Wasowski

THE CONTEMPORARY GARDENER

CB

CONTEMPORARY BOOKS

Library of Congress Cataloging-in-Publication Data

Wasowski, Andy, 1939–.
    The landscaping revolution : garden with mother nature, not against her / Andy Wasowski and Sally Wasowski.
        p.   cm. — (The Contemporary Gardener)
    Includes bibliographical references (p.   ).
    ISBN 0-8092-2665-0
    1. Natural landscaping.   2. Native plant gardening.
    3. Natural gardens.   I. Wasowski, Sally, 1946–
    II. Title   III. Series.
    SB439.W367   2000
    635.9′5173—dc21
                                                    99-23152
                                                      CIP

THE CONTEMPORARY GARDENER

Other books in the Contemporary Gardener series:
Gaining Ground, Maureen Gilmer
Gardening Wisdom, Doug Green
Growing Perennials in Cold Climates, Mike Heger and John Whitman
Growing Roses in Cold Climates, Jerry Olson and John Whitman

Interior design by Hespenheide Design
Interior photographs by Andy Wasowski

Published by Contemporary Books
A division of NTC/Contemporary Publishing Group, Inc.
4255 West Touhy Avenue, Lincolnwood (Chicago), Illinois 60646-1975 U.S.A.
Copyright © 2000 by Andy Wasowski and Sally Wasowski
All rights reserved. No part of this book may be reproduced, stored in a retrieval system, or transmitted in any form or by any means, electronic, mechanical, photocopying, recording, or otherwise, without the prior written permission of NTC/Contemporary Publishing Group, Inc.
Printed and bound in Hong Kong by Midas Printing Company
International Standard Book Number: 0-8092-2665-0

18   17   16   15   14   13   12   11   10   9   8   7   6   5   4   3   2   1

For Sally: wife, colleague, playmate, teacher, best friend

Also by Andy and Sally Wasowski

Native Landscaping from El Paso to L.A.

Native Texas Plants: Landscaping Region by Region

Requiem for a Lawnmower

Gardening with Native Plants of the South

Native Texas Gardens: Maximum Beauty, Minimum Upkeep

Gardening with Prairie: How to Create Beautiful and Earth-Friendly Landscapes

Building Inside Nature's Envelope

"I feel a sense of urgency when I see the fields and wild meadows of yesteryear turning into a grid of shopping malls, a spaghetti network of highways, and houses chockablock in subdivisions. If we don't incorporate native plants into our planned landscapes, we might forfeit this precious heritage."

Lady Bird Johnson

"Too often we are unwilling to look beyond ourselves to see the effect of our actions today on our children and grandchildren."

Vice President Al Gore

"I firmly believe that by the second decade of the new century, native landscaping will become the norm, and that the typical highly controlled landscape of today will be viewed as a museum piece . . . a symbol of our wasteful past. And it could happen sooner."

Dr. David Northington
Former Executive Director
Lady Bird Johnson Wildflower Center

TABLE OF CONTENTS

ACKNOWLEDGMENTS

How do I list all the people who have influenced me, taught me, and inspired me over a span of almost two decades? The list would number in the hundreds, and even then would probably leave out some very worthy people. Instead, I've decided that the one person above all others who deserves my thanks and appreciation is my wife, Sally.

After over thirty years in the advertising business, I knew I was ripe for a change of direction. She gave it to me. One day, she asked me to "help out a little" on a book she wanted to write—not because she was interested in becoming a literary lioness, but because, as a landscape designer, she needed something to show clients—a book that would not only profile various native plants, but also show how they can be used in home landscapes. No such book existed. Sally decided to remedy that situation, and I wound up shooting the photos, rewriting

her prose, driving the van, and contributing my most valuable asset—my ignorance. She claims that I kept her on target by periodically asking the kind of questions lay readers would likely ask: "Wait, what does that mean? Isn't there a simpler way to say this?" If I knew even half of what she knows, I'd be out of a job.

Over the years, our partnership has worked because we know our individual strengths and weaknesses, and happily discovered that we complement each other. She is the plant expert and designer, I am the generalist. It has worked, and she's the best (and toughest) boss I ever had.

I must also give a big thanks to our agent, Jeanne Fredericks, and to our editor, Anne Knudsen, and the staff at NTC/Contemporary, who turned my manuscript into this very handsome tome: Julia Anderson, Nancy Hall, Kim Bartko, and Gigi Grajdura.

"The average American homeowner would rather
live next to a pervert, heroin-addict, communist
pornographer than someone with an unkempt lawn."
Dave Barry

INTRODUCTION

Let's have a show of hands . . .

Who didn't even know there *was* a landscaping revolution going on? Probably most of you. After all, when you look around your neighborhood, everything still looks pretty much the same as it always has—the shrubs are neatly trimmed, the sprinklers are anointing the turf grass with lots of H_2O, and so far you haven't spotted anyone marching outside the local garden center carrying picket signs denouncing lawn mowers and pesticides.

The traditional American landscape—manicured lawn, geometrically clipped box hedges, and rows of exotic posies lined up like cadets on parade—seems to be, at least for now, safe and secure. The dominant weekend sound in any typical suburban neighborhood continues to be, not the shouts and laughter of children at play, but the eardrum-shattering cacophony of power mowers, power edgers, power pruners, and surely the most diabolical of all, power leaf blowers! (It's my firm opinion that the lowest and hottest level in the netherworld has been reserved for its inventor!)

At this point, I should probably clear up one point: when I carry on about all that work we put into our landscapes, I am not talking about dedicated gardeners—hobbyists

This is the typical American landscape. It looks simple enough. So how come we spend so much time taking care of it? And why does it look like a boring clone of virtually every other landscape from coast to coast? No wonder a landscaping revolution has been taking place all over the country.

who happily and creatively spend many hours a week among their flowers. For them, this is therapy, recreation, and artistic expression. (These gardeners, by the way, are certainly not excluded from being part of this revolution. They will simply begin using plants that are far better suited to their locales than the ones they have been using.)

I'm talking about the average homeowner who, as a rule, does not consider him- or herself to be a "gardener." They might not know a coreopsis from a conifer, and may think that a ground cover is what they pull over the infield when it rains. For some, the closest they get to actual gardening is owning a Chia Pet! Ask them, and they'll rattle off a list of things they'd rather be doing than mowing. All they want is an attractive landscape that they don't have to spend every weekend maintaining.

How do I know? Because, not all that long ago, I was one of them. The job of keeping the turf tamed around the humble New Jersey homestead where I grew up fell to me at an early age—ten or eleven as I recall. In fact, I actually thought it was something of an honor—a rite of passage from kidhood into young manhood. Then I discovered two things: the precipitous slope at the front of the house (great for sledding, lousy for mowing), and the fact that the family push mower weighed more than I did. The honor rapidly degenerated and, had I been aware of child labor laws, I would probably have placed a call in to the state attorney general. This "honor" remained mine until I graduated from college, at which point I bolted for a bachelor apartment where they paid people to mow the grass.

But my respite was relatively short-lived. One day I looked up and found myself not only married but a suburban homeowner, with a backyard that seemed to be large enough to accommodate polo matches. As I dutifully tended to the needs of this sprawling expanse of Kentucky blue, I found myself wondering if it might be possible to retroac-

tively add "I won't do yard work" to the marriage vows. At that time, I hadn't heard anything about any landscaping revolution, but if I had, believe-you-me, I would have been marching in the first rank. Ten years later, I finally got the word. But more about that in a later chapter.

If you're a typical American homeowner, then you know from personal experience that owning a lawn-centered landscape (or is it the other way around!?) demands continual supervision and upkeep. After all, it exists on an artificial life-support system. It couldn't go on without you. Ignore it for a month or two and you no longer have a landscape. As a result, you must commit to toiling long hours under a sweltering sun, pouring oceans of water on your landscape, and making repeated trips to your garden center—as well as repeated trips to your wallet—for seed and sod, herbicides and pesticides, and a wide assortment of gardening paraphernalia, replacement plants, and those all-important how-to books. This is no penny-ante operation; according to the Lawn Care Institute, turf and lawn maintenance (for homes, golf courses, the spacious grounds of corporate headquarters, etc.) is a $27 billion a year industry. That's ten times more than we spend on school textbooks!

Ultimately, of course, even the most insensitive homeowner must ask, how has the traditional American landscape really benefited us? Call me a cynic, but I suspect the answer is, by earning us the approval of our neighbors. The unpleasant truth of the matter is, we go through all this, not so much for ourselves, but for the Joneses and Ginsbergs up and down the block. We, and they, view it as sacrosanct. The manicured lawn-centered landscape has been the norm for so long that we've come to think of it as being as American as baseball, apple pie, and Ozzie and Harriet. Moreover, there are those who, when confronted with the option of getting rid of their lawns, react with something akin to horror.

We've got this friend who is forever complaining about how hard it is for her to maintain her lawn—she has to do it because her husband flat-out refuses. "So get rid of the lawn," I said, not unreasonably. Boy, you should have seen the look of horror she gave me. It was inconceivable to her that she not have turf grass around her home. You'd have thought that I'd suggested she sell her daughter into the white slavery market!

Horror isn't the only reaction you get. Even more common is the one we got from a former neighbor back in Dallas. For over a dozen years, he lived across the street from us and our naturalistic landscape, and at least once a year he'd comment on how lovely it was and how he enjoyed watching it change with the seasons. This, mind you, while he was out pushing his lawn mower under that merciless Texas summer sun. More than once, I mentioned that a naturalistic landscape such as ours—the one he so admired—would be a lot less work (are you detecting a certain missionary zeal here?), and each time he'd shake his head and chortle self-consciously and say, "Oh, well, that's just not for me." What he was saying, of course, was that it was OK for *some* folks to do wild and crazy things—like eat arugula salad and go on vacation to Costa Rica—but he was just an average Joe and he'd stick with iceberg lettuce and Orlando, thank you very much.

Revolution? you ask. Where? And who?

Trust me, it's going on. Maybe not on your block, but somewhere nearby. All over this country, homeowners are taking a hard look at their landscapes, and they're having epiphanies. They're saying, "Hey, who needs all this work? Who needs to be dumping all this precious water on the zinnias and marigolds? Who needs the smell of chemicals in the grass?"

They are realizing that landscaping can no longer be seen as a war between Mother Nature and us. They are grasping the simple fact that we cannot continue to obliterate wildlife habitats to make room for shopping malls and subdivisions; we have to start giving something back by creating sanctuaries for these displaced creatures around our homes.

They are understanding that in a landscape that imitates the principles of nature, there is balance and beauty; most problems

© John Branch, *San Antonio-Express News*

When people actually see native plants used in landscape situations, misconceptions about "weediness" and undesirability quickly evaporate. Here, at Cheekwood Gardens, in Nashville, Tennessee, visitors can stroll through native fall color and get an idea how it might look around their own homes.

take care of themselves. And that gardening can no longer be viewed as merely a matter of aesthetics or conforming to arbitrary neighborhood standards. *Today, gardening and environmental responsibility must go hand in hand.*

In these pages, you're going to meet some of these landscaping revolutionaries, and find out what motivated them to join the natural landscaping movement. You're also going to discover a variety of revolutionary ideas about what to do with the ground around your domicile—and why it's important to change your long-held ideas about what constitutes a "respectable" landscape.

And, you're going to learn how you, too, can become a landscaping revolutionary. You'll learn to work *with* Mother Nature, not against her. You'll learn commonsense approaches to gardening that will make you wonder why you've never looked at your yard that way before. We humans like to think of ourselves as a rational species. But when you consider how we've been landscaping for the past century and a half, you have to wonder if that's really true. But first, let's take a quick look at what's been going on with this revolution.

Report from the Front Lines

For starters, it's a movement still in its infancy. Ah, but what an infant! Consider just a few of the many examples of how quickly it has grown since the early 1980s.

- National gardening publications (*Fine Gardening, Horticulture, The American Gardener*, etc.) that rarely if ever mentioned natives in the past, now routinely include features on native gardening in every issue. This is also true for gardening programs on radio and television.
- A growing library of related and successful books by respected authors such as Sara Stein, Ken Druse, Carole Otteson,

Janet Marinelli, Leslie Sauer, Jim Wilson, Judith Meilke, and others, promotes native/natural landscaping.

- In 1994, President Clinton issued a presidential directive stating that all federal buildings and installations should landscape with plants native to their areas. This directive has met with widespread acceptance.

- Virtually every state has a native plant society, or some related organization, and they are adding chapters and members all the time. California, with thirty active chapters, has a membership exceeding ten thousand. Texas has thirty-one chapters, while the Wild Ones, which began in Milwaukee in 1979 and is dedicated to promoting natural landscaping, currently has twenty-two chapters in eleven states and carries on a vigorous expansion program. By the time you read this book, they may very well have doubled their numbers.

- Master Gardeners and other garden clubs are now embracing the concept of environmental gardening and adding native landscaping to their programs.

- Significantly, nurseries that specialize in native plants have gone from a mere handful fifteen years ago to many hundreds. It's difficult to maintain an updated list of these invaluable resources because, it seems, new ones appear on the scene every day. These nurseries could not exist without widespread consumer interest. As one nursery owner once told me, "I can only sell what people will buy. This business is too hard for me to be a pioneer promoting plants that people don't want." Moreover, business is good. In Florida alone, native plants have become a $101 million-per-year industry.

- The Lady Bird Johnson Wildflower Center in Austin, Texas (formerly called the National Wildflower Research Center), draws over one hundred thousand visitors annually.

- Native demonstration gardens are now an important and popular part of most botanic gardens and arboreta around the country: Cheekwood Gardens in Nashville, Calloway Gardens in Georgia, Morton Arboretum in Chicago, Phoenix Botanic Gardens, and Strybing Arboretum and Botanical Garden in San Francisco, to name a few. Others, such as Rancho Santa Ana Botanic Gardens in Claremont, California, Garden in the Woods in Framingham, Massachusetts, and the Sonoran Desert Museum in Tucson, Arizona, are dedicated exclusively to natives.

- Water departments all over the country are promoting *xeriscaping*, a technique for water conservation that makes native plants an important part of its program.

- The expanding interest in native plants in America has even been noticed abroad. In her recent report to the Winston Churchill Memorial Trust, Dr. Helen Shaw wrote that "*In North America, a natural garden/landscape movement, which advocates the use of indigenous plants for landscaping around the home, has been growing steadily in size and stature. Moreover, an increasing number of garden and landscape designers have chosen to adopt this more naturalistic approach and are committed to finding a new direction for the American landscape.*" Dr. Shaw concludes that a similar approach is badly needed in Great Britain.

The landscaping revolution is alive and well, thank you, and growing more vigorous and enthusiastic with each passing day. The native plant movement represents the cutting edge of gardening. It is not hyperbole to say that this landscaping revolution is going to be *the* gardening trend for the new century.

When the sound of bulldozers is heard in the distance, native plant societies organize plant rescues—fast. One of the most active rescue operations is run by Jeane Reeves of the Georgia Native Plant Society. Plants that have been saved are then donated to organizations that promise to plant and care for these botanical treasures.

Field trips, plant rescues, and public education are just a few of the many outreach programs native plant societies undertake. Today, most states have an organization dedicated to promoting native landscaping. For a current list, see the appendix.

Chapter 1

THE BIRTH OF THE LEMON LANDSCAPE

Thrill of the Grass. **Just call Richard Widmark "Lawnmower Man." The actor told** *Architectural Digest* **about his passion for cutting grass. He mows the 40 acres of his Connecticut estate, plus the lawns of his neighbors. "Mowing is very satisfying," he said. "It's all about wanting everything to be neat and under control."**

AP wire, 1991

U nder control! That, in a nutshell, is what's wrong with the typical American landscape. It is so under control, it has become extremely labor intensive, very unfriendly to the environment, and remarkably boring!

Yet we persist in coddling it and spending a good portion of our free time seeing to its every need—slaves to what writer Sara Lowen calls "The tyranny of the lawn." Which strikes me as more than odd. If I rounded up everybody I know who enjoys landscape maintenance, they would fit comfortably into the back seat of a Yugo, and still leave room for a bentwood rocker, two stereo speakers, and a mature Rottweiler.

So, after reading that AP blurb about Mr. Widmark and his quirky fascination with turf

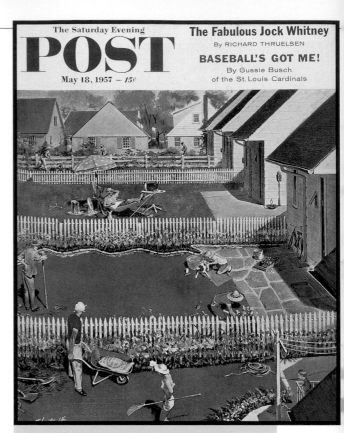

The Saturday Evening **POST**
May 18, 1957 — *15¢*

The Fabulous Jock Whitney
By RICHARD THRUELSEN

BASEBALL'S GOT ME!
By Gussie Busch
of the St. Louis Cardinals

Nothing epitomized its time and place better than the old *Saturday Evening Post*. In this 1957 Thorton Utz cover, we see a suburban scene where one heretical home-owner chooses not to join his neighbors in their weekend landscape ritual; he's actually relaxing with a cool drink and enjoying himself! How un-American can you get!?

We have this thing about being in control. It drives us to grow sun-loving grass under shade trees, acid-loving azaleas in alka-line soil, and yes, even banana trees in Kansas. Why do we think we can do it better than Mother Nature?

trimming, I rushed to my local library to read the full text of that *Architectural Digest* profile, hoping for some deeper insight into his curious predilection. What I read only served to confound me further. The article recounted how, one day, Mr. Widmark cut his foot rather severely on his mower. And guess what his first words to the doctor were? Not "When can I act again?" but "When can I mow again?"

Are you so afflicted? Consider this:

What if your car needed a tune-up every month, an oil change every week, and the tires rebalanced every five hundred miles (805 km)? You'd call it a lemon and get rid of it—fast! Now, consider that your very own traditional American landscape demands watering two or three times a week all summer, mowing once or twice a week, periodic pruning, lots of weeding, and ongoing applications of herbicides, pesticides, and artificial fertilizers.

Face it, my friend, that landscape is a sun-ripened, grade-A, all-American lemon.

It's Genetic!

How did we acquire this affinity for well-manicured landscapes? According to John Falk, a Maryland biologist, it all began millions of years ago, back when our Pleistocene ancestors were romping around the savannas of Africa. It isn't hard to imagine why being surrounded by short grass was an asset in the survival game; it allowed these early humans to spot predators long before they got within nibbling range. Falk believes that this primeval experience, repeated for myriad generations, resulted in our being encoded *genetically* with a preference for short grass!

And that means *all* of us. Falk conducted surveys all over the world and discovered that cultivated lawns have been around from ancient Persia to the present day, and exist from Passaic, New Jersey, to Hyderabad, India. (An earlier book by my wife and me, *Requiem for a Lawnmower*, actually sold five copies in Saudi Arabia!)

Moving up in time to seventeenth- and eighteenth-century Europe, we note that virtually every locale had some big shot with a title, such as earl or duke or prince, and he lived in a large castle or manor house. Which was surrounded by . . . a lawn. This was his not-so-subtle way of telling the peasants who worked for him (and lived in somewhat more reduced circumstances) that he didn't need this land for mundane things like farming. He was rich and could afford to literally waste his land by planting it with an unproductive lawn. And he didn't have to worry about the upkeep; that's what the sheep and the serfs were for. It was nothing less than an ostentatious display of one-upmanship.

This was not lost on the serfs, of course, and in future generations, when millions would immigrate to this country seeking their own fortunes, the concept of "every man's

How to explain our affinity for lawns? One biologist thinks it may well be genetic—the result of our Pleistocene ancestors realizing that short grass allowed them to see predators coming. It was all about survival. Short grass, good. Tall grass, bad!

Peter Bianchi © National Geographic Society

Do you see a lawn in front of this re-creation of an early colonial home? Of course not. The first Europeans to arrive on our shores were plenty busy enough just surviving. Photo taken at the Jamestown Settlement in Virginia.

home (no matter how humble) is his castle" was born. And with those "castles" came lawns—just like the big shots had.

In his 1899 work, *The Theory of the Working Class*, Thorstein Veblen described the lawn as an example of conspicuous consumption. Land was a valued commodity, so covering it with an unproductive lawn was seen as the epitome of having made it big-time.

But, of course, there is more to the lemon landscape than grass. It is also composed of trees, shrubs, annuals, and perennials, and they too require a good deal of upkeep.

And to explain why we put up with this labor, we must again look back in history. When the northern Europeans first arrived on these shores, they soon discovered that it wasn't going to be easy establishing a toehold in this often hostile country. They had to cope with harsh weather, crop failures, swamp fever, and ongoing conflicts with the

indigenous people who, understandably, weren't terribly thrilled to be evicted from their ancestral lands by these pushy palefaces.

It was a hardscrabble way of life, and whatever gardening was being done by our ancestors was focused on raising food to eat. Only later, when three square meals a day became the norm and each community could boast a school, a library, and a few churches, did these hearty settlers look around and say, "Hey, we're not frontier anymore. We're civilized!"

At that point, they began gardening for aesthetic reasons. And what they desired above all was to have "civilized" gardens—to reflect their hard-won new station in life. To do this, they naturally looked to the civilized gardens they were already familiar with back from whence they had come—for the most part, northern Europe. And later, when our itchy-footed ancestors moved west, and went

There came a day when the colonists felt they had established a "civilized" society—and could now afford to garden for aesthetic reasons. Naturally, they copied the gardens they'd known back in the Old Country, with plants that were native to other parts of the world.

flowers such as hollyhocks and carnations. And they didn't give one second's thought to whether or not these imported plants would like their new homes. In most cases, they did not. These plants weren't stupid. They understood very quickly that Georgia didn't have a lot in common—vegetationally speaking—with Nottingham or Leeds, and New Mexico was not a carbon copy of New England.

But never mind. The newly civilized settlers just sent for more of the same. And the companies that shipped the European stock to the New World must have gotten filthy rich on the continuing reorders.

As for all the colorful and hearty native flora that were thriving all about—right under the noses of these settlers—well, these were considered to be weeds, not fit to be included in a civilized garden with the exotics.

There were exceptions. Native trees, such as flowering dogwood, redbud, southern magnolia, American elm, and sugar maple were deemed to be acceptable, especially as they were often already established on the property. And a few natives, such as Virginia creeper, Turk's cap, pink evening primrose, and Queen of the Prairie were used in pioneer gardens.

Paradoxically, the real horticultural work on American native plants was done in

The rugged souls who settled the Old West thought that whatever they could grow in New England would grow in New Mexico or Texas or the Dakotas just as well. The chief beneficiaries of this kind of thinking were the seed companies and the shipping companies who got rich sending out replacements. Today, not much has changed. Standard nursery stock is still composed mainly of imports that are unsuited to wherever they are expected to thrive.

through the same routine establishing themselves in the prairie states, the western mountains, and the deserts of the Southwest, they looked back fondly to their gardens in New England and the Carolinas, and imported all the old and familiar water-craving European and Asian planting stock they had used before.

They imported seeds and saplings by the wagon load and planted their gardens with cedar of Lebanon and English boxwood, and

Urban Myth

A friend recently told me something that I immediately mentally filed under "urban myths." He said he'd heard that city dwellers in Manhattan high-rises were growing little patches of lawn in their apartments! Not out on the balconies, mind you, but inside. I immediately called a gardening editor I knew in New York City and was informed that, yes indeed, my friend's story was true. I was told that these lawns were on the smallish side—no croquet playing here!—but the containers ranged from simple eight-by-ten-inch (20-by-25cm) wooden boxes to larger, more elaborate versions.

Witness the Urban Gardener's Table from Smith & Hawken. They call it the "Central Park of coffee tables" and "An oasis of greenery." This birch veneer table has a watertight aluminum insert that people fill with potting soil and then sprinkle with the grass seed of their choice. The table is then rolled—on industrial-strength casters—next to a window or beneath a grow light, and watered from time to time. The resulting crop of turf is "mowed," I assume, with scissors. The price? A mere $750!

The urban "lawn" as a coffee-table centerpiece, as seen in the Spring 1988 Smith & Hawken catalog. Too tiny for croquet, but maybe you could wiggle your toes in the grass—one foot at a time.

Europe and Japan. New England aster, New Belgium aster, heath aster, sundrops *Oenothera tetragona*, the white obedient plant *Physostegia virginiana*, numerous cultivars of *Phlox paniculata*, spiderwort, sweet gum, tulip tree, honey locust, and the elegant sorrel tree *Oxydendrum aroboreum*, have long been favorites in English gardens. But it took centuries for us to appreciate our own native plants, and then did so only with a foreign seal of approval. In 1744 *Monarda didyma* went to Europe and in this century finally came home as 'Cambridge Scarlet.' *Rudbeckia laciniata* crossed the ocean in 1640 and didn't return until 1990 as the hybrid 'Herbstsonne.' *Eustoma grandiflora* eventually made its way to Japan and came back as the gorgeous hybrid bedding plant and cut flower *Lisianthus*. Unfortunately, on its complex horticultural journey, *Lisianthus* lost its drought-tolerance and its ability to make vital seed.

Today, of course, we aren't doing things very differently. Most homeowners still ignore their native flora, and rely instead on the imported species sold at their neighborhood nursery.

Frank J. Scott, a Cincinnati landscape architect, was largely responsible for our present mind-set about neatly manicured lawns. His 1870 book, *The Art of Beautifying Suburban Home Grounds*, became the bible for America's homeowners—and today we're still stuck with his ideas.

Blame It All on Frank

The lemon landscape got a big push at the end of the last century when various "experts" decreed what the home landscape should look like. In 1870, landscape architect Frank J. Scott (no relation to the seed company), came out with a book that was soon the gardening "bible" for homeowners all over America. Called *The Art of Beautifying Suburban Home Grounds*, Scott's tome stated that "A smooth closely shaven surface of grass is by far the most essential element of beauty on the grounds of a suburban home."

And, yes Virginia, there was such a place as suburbia way back then. It wasn't very large compared to what we have today—usually just a few blocks of homes immediately adjacent to downtown.

In 1830, an English textile engineer named Edwin Budding had a brainstorm while observing a rotary shear used to trim the nap on carpets, and one of the very first lawn mowers was developed. In applying for his patent, Budding enthused, "Country gentlemen will find in using my machine an amusing and healthful exercise." Unfortunately for Budding, there wasn't much demand for his product. Wrong decade, and to a large measure, wrong country. The grass-carpeted front yard was very much an American phenomenon and, as Virginia Scott Jenkins observed in her book, *The Lawn: A History of an American Obsession*, visitors to this country in the late nineteenth century often commented on this "strange element in American landscapes."

The first U.S. patent for a lawn mower was issued in 1868. By 1881, the United States Patent Office had issued 138 patents (who'd have thought there could have been so many distinct variations!), and manufacturers had produced 47,661 of them. (The first lawn sprinkler, by the way, got its U.S. patent in 1871, so clearly the lemon landscape was well established long before the advent of the twentieth century.)

mowers came on the scene—along with another newfangled contraption, the automobile. A 1916 ad for one of the early power mowers announced that "it eliminates the nuisance of a horse-drawn contrivance on your lawn." That mower, by the way, cost $225—a pretty high price for the average working stiff in those days.

But it was a price he willingly paid. Conformity in landscaping was deemed

These rotary-bladed push mowers made adherence to Mr. Scott's dictum possible. As one garden writer observed in 1875, "Since the introduction of the lawn-mowers, the keeping of the lawn has been so simplified that no suburban residence is complete without one."

Still, it was a lot of work. These newfangled mowers, while easier to manage than the scythe, were heavy and cumbersome. So, by the end of the nineteenth century, power

essential. In his book, *Gardening for Pleasure* (1875), Peter Henderson made it quite clear what he thought of homeowners who did not conform: "It is gratifying to know that such neighbors are not numerous, for the example of the majority will soon shame them into decency."

During the late nineteenth and early twentieth centuries, the lemon landscape increased in public acceptance. When the Democratic National Convention came to

Kansas City in 1900, the powers that be set about to beautify their community, and gave prizes for the best-maintained lawns and flower gardens. The Tree Planting and Foundation Association of Brooklyn, New York, encouraged residents to convert their courtyards into manicured grassy plots, and also talked the city fathers into taking out the old flagstones that surrounded city hall and replacing them with lawn.

A major influence in popularizing the lawn-centered landscape was the Garden Clubs of America, which educated homeowners on how to grow the ideal lawn and developed programs to foster aesthetic appreciation for neatly carpeted front yards.

One of the biggest influences in popularizing lawns was, believe it or not, the U.S. Golf Association. Interestingly, golf and the "perfect lawn" concept grew hand in hand. Amateur golfers couldn't help but notice the well-maintained grass they played on, and began to develop higher standards for their own home turf. Naturally, they turned, not to landscapers or gardening experts, but to golf course managers. A 1926 ad for Toro lawn mowers advised readers to "ask the Greenskeeper at your own club what he thinks of Toro equipment." Other ads for lawn products promoted the "golf course look" as the ideal for home lawns. In later years, PGA stars such as Sam Sneed, Arnold Palmer, and Jack Nicklaus touted lawn-care products in magazine ads and on TV.

During the Second World War, Americans were deprived of much of the help they had become used to from the lawn-care industry. Lawn mower manufacturers were engaged in making equipment for the armed forces, fertilizer companies were making munitions, and the makers of pesticides and other lawn chemicals were making poison gas! Many still continued to advertise, however, telling their old customers that they were doing their patriotic duty but they'd be back at the old stand when the hostilities

In the late '40s and early '50s, Madison Avenue was there to promote the ideal lawn-centered landscape, and made certain that American homeowners knew exactly what was expected of them. The landscape industry was growing by leaps and bounds, thanks to the great postwar move to suburbia. By 1937, we were spending $100 million a year on our lawns; today, according to the National Gardening Association, we spend almost $7 billion annually on home lawn-care equipment and products.

were over. One such ad proclaimed, "Your 1943 Coldwell mower is riding the convoy lanes somewhere on the high seas . . ." But lest their readers get the idea that fighting this war was a bad idea, the company hastened to add, "The new ideas and methods we are learning everyday assure you of the finest lawn mowers obtainable in the future."

The end of World War II really sparked the expansion of the lemon landscape. And not a minute too soon; an article in *Home and Garden* magazine lamented that "The lawn is one of the saddest wartime casualties." But now that it was all over over there, the lemon landscape would be back bigger and better than ever.

The chemical and munitions industries, freed from their wartime responsibilities, turned to manufacturing and promoting lawn chemicals and fertilizers. And did they have a ready market! In 1945, millions of servicemen and women came home, got discharged, got married, and got mortgages. There was an immediate need in the country for 5 million new homes, and builders responded, led by William Levitt, the inventor of the mass-produced subdivision. First in Long Island, and a few years later in Pennsylvania, Levitt provided the American dream for just $6,990 and only $100 down! By 1955, three out of four new homes in America were being built on his mass-produced subdivision concept — rows upon rows of look-alike but affordable homes that sported yard after yard of look-alike lawn-centered landscapes.

Peter Henderson's comment in 1875 about conformity was just as true in post–World War II America—and still is today.

Lawns not only surround our homes, they surround where we work, where we go to school, where we worship, where we play. And if that isn't bad enough, when we die they stick a lawn on *top* of us!

Chapter 2

YOUR LAWN HAS A DRINKING PROBLEM

"Surely then, we
humans, with all
our knowledge and
logic, would con-
serve water and not
foul it."

Gordon K. Durnil
*The Making of a
Conservative
Environmentalist*

What sparked the landscaping revolution? In a word, water. There came a day when people began to wake up to the fact that our world's water supply is not infinite . . . in fact, it's quite fragile. It isn't that we don't have enough water; four-fifths of our planet's surface area is covered with the stuff. Trouble is, 97 percent of it is seawater. Salty. Unfit for agriculture, drinking, and yes, even watering that lemon landscape. Only 3 percent is fresh water, and two-thirds of that is locked up in glaciers and icecaps, or in underground reserves that, so far, have been economically unfeasible to tap. Put another way, if all the water on earth were represented by a gallon jug, all our fresh, useable water could be held by just one tablespoon.

The amount of water we have today is the amount we had when *Tyrannosaurus rex* was stomping around. The water we drink today is the same water *Australopithecus* drank. The same water Hannibal's legions drank. The same water Confucius, Catherine the Great, and Charlie Chaplin all drank. Recycled a couple of zillion times, of course, but let's not dwell on that!

One way we're recycling water is desalination. This process of taking impure salt water and converting it into fresh water has been around for a very long time, and consisted of boiling seawater and collecting the pure condensation. "Modern" techniques have been in use for about half a century, with 10,300 desalination plants worldwide today—although four-fifths of them treat brackish water, not seawater. And while it's deemed to be friendly to the environment, it's still a very expensive process. The city council of Port Hueneme, California, raised water rates 271 percent to pay for their badly needed desalination plant. In the arid Middle East, where for some reason they insist on growing melons and other crops that are highly water dependent, farmers who rely on desalinated water must be heavily subsidized by their governments.

Subsidizing the cost of water is not limited to the Middle East or to desalination efforts. Much of our own household water is subsidized, making it the best deal in your household budget. So how come you aren't paying what water is really worth? Because too many communities are still hung up on that old chamber of commerce Growth Is Good mentality. To bring in industry and more residents to work in those companies, they keep water rates artificially low so nobody gets scared off. They can't have anyone thinking that there isn't enough water here to support all this expansion. "Look at our beautiful golf courses. Look at the bubbling fountains in front of the convention center. Water? No problem! We've got oceans of it!" Meanwhile, these municipalities are scrambling like mad to buy, beg, borrow, and steal every drop they can get their pipelines on, diverting from there to get it over here.

But the bubble has to burst one day. A recent TV special on the history of Las Vegas ended on the ominous note that in a hundred years the desert would reclaim all those bright lights and fountain displays, and we'll have to go elsewhere to lose our money.

© John Trevor, *Albuquerque Journal Tribune*

NOW THAT WE'VE RESTORED PROSPERITY, LET'S PASS A MINIMUM-RAINFALL BILL TO END THE WESTERN DROUGHT....

The Rain Drain

Our planet gets some 4 trillion gallons (15 trillion L) of rainfall every day. You'd think

Visitors to Las Vegas may be excused for forgetting they're in the middle of a desert when they see extravagant water displays such as this. And, while this water is recycled, groundwater must still be used in the community for more mundane purposes, such as doing the laundry, cooking meals, and watering landscapes. In some parts of the Las Vegas Valley, groundwater levels have dropped around five feet (1.5 m), while annual rainfall to replenish these stressed supplies totals a mere four inches (10 cm). As the city grows (four thousand new residents per month), can its water supply keep up? By the end of the next century, will sand and tumbleweed fill the streets where tourists now teem?

that would be enough to quench our insatiable thirst. But most of that water is lost due to evaporation and runoff. What sticks around, we do our best to destroy with pollution. In one of his television documentaries, Jacques Cousteau revisited an area of the Mediterranean Sea he had filmed back in the early 1950s. Then, the water was lush with vegetation and animal life. When he returned, thirty-odd years later, he filmed an undersea desert—a wasteland created by sewage and toxic waste, devoid of fish and plants.

But don't go blaming it all on heartless, insensitive industrialists. We don't do such a hot job handling hazardous wastes in our own homes. All too often, everything from nail-polish remover and paint strippers to motor oil and antifreeze simply gets poured down the drain and into our water supply.

The aquifers that many communities depend on for water are also endangered—not just by pollution, but by development. In the Hill Country of Texas, the aquifers of the Edwards Plateau, which are replenished by rainwater seeping down through the limestone, are threatened because the land has been covered by shopping malls, parking lots, office complexes, and other seep-proof obstacles. Playa lakes, which cover the Texas Panhandle, and neighboring areas in Colorado, Oklahoma, New Mexico, and Kansas, are threatened by agricultural chemicals that drain down into these wetlands. The playas, a valuable wildlife habitat, are believed to recharge the High Plains Ogallala aquifer—the source of approximately 30 percent of this country's groundwater.

Then, too, it doesn't always rain on schedule—and almost never when and where you really need it. We've always had droughts, but we got hit by some biggies back in the '70s and '80s, and that really got our attention. In 1978, water rates in New Mexico quadrupled. By 1988, when the Midwest was especially hard hit, water departments were reporting that in some western states 75 percent of their annual water consumption was poured on their lawns.

During the summer of 1999, much of the country went through a prolonged hot spell with daytime temperatures going over 100 degrees Fahrenheit (38 degrees Celsius) for weeks on end, and no rain in sight.

Besides periodic droughts, pollution, salinity, and endangered aquifers, our water problems are aggravated by the simple fact that, while our water supply isn't growing, our population and our demands on that water supply are. It took us from the beginning of time to around 1835 to propagate a billion people. Today, we add a billion thirsty people to the planet every fifteen years.

Slaking That Thirst

No wonder people began to look for ways to conserve this precious commodity. One very good way, they realized, was to change the way they landscaped. And that meant rethinking the lawn.

Now, let's put this in perspective. Our water crisis—and don't kid yourself, it *is* a crisis—is a highly complex, global issue. And nobody is saying that by changing our landscaping practices, we're going to solve it. But we can help it. A lot. Certainly, by continuing the way we've been going, we can only make the problem worse.

There are, after all, over 30 million acres (12 million ha) of lawn in the U.S., which is the equivalent of mowing the entire state of Alabama every Saturday. That much sod also requires a lot of water! A twenty-five-by-forty-foot (8-by-12-m) lawn needs ten thousand gallons (37,850 L) each summer. On average, homeowners pour from 40 to 60 percent of their household water on lawns, shrubs, and bedding plants. Incredibly, some of the most verdant lawns I've seen were in desert communities such as El Paso, Phoenix, Las Vegas, and Palm Springs, where they get as little as four to twelve inches (10 to 30 cm) of rain annually. Drive through neighbor-

Everything goes with the house but the lawn. They're taking that with them.

© Vahan Shirvanian

Ever wonder why there are so many lawns in the arid Southwest? To a large extent, it's because we are a very mobile society. And when folks move to new and unfamiliar parts of the country, they want to take a little of what's familiar along with them. They know they can't pack up and move Al and Sadie next door, whom they've been buddies with since forever. And that quaint little Italian café they were so fond of will also have to be left behind. Ah, but they *can* take their landscapes—at least in a figurative sense. So, when folks from North Carolina or Kansas move out to Arizona, before you know it, they've installed back-home-style landscapes all around their new homes. Never mind that these lawn-centered landscapes are totally inappropriate to their new surroundings.

hoods in these cities in August and you'll see the sprinklers going full blast at high noon, with much of that precious water evaporating into the air or running down the street.

Of course, for most folks, giving up their lawns was simply unthinkable. So other options were explored. People started putting bricks in their toilet tanks to save water, and some communities touted the "Two-Minute Shower."

To cater to a more water-conscious public, companies began designing and selling more efficient lawn irrigation systems: check valves, drip irrigation, rain guards, moisture meters, and other high-tech devices were soon on the market. Some communities have introduced "water cops," whose main job is to patrol neighborhoods and ticket homeowners who overwater their lawns and allow runoff to escape into the street. This program also created a new kind of citizen—the water snitch, who reports his or her neighbors' watering abuses.

And California homeowners can now hire people to come out and spray biodegradable green paint on their parched lawns—conserving water while maintaining an acceptably verdant look that Frank J. Scott would have approved.

Over the years, homeowners have devised some innovative water-conserving alternatives of their own. Green concrete is a perennial favorite; others prefer gravel in a variety of pastel hues, bordered by painted bricks or rocks—the Sun City look. And a few even resort to Astroturf. Admittedly, while all of these get high marks for water conservation—not to mention low maintenance—they come up short in the aesthetics department. Besides, these options are . . . well . . . dead! Most of us want living alternatives.

It's Not Zero-Scape!

In 1981, the Denver Water Department joined the landscaping revolution. They were actually recruited by the president of the Associated Landscape Contractors of Colorado, Jim Grabow. He asked them to see what they could come up with to make landscape water use more efficient. What they came up with was a concept they called *xeriscaping*. The term was coined by Nancy Leavitt, an environmental planner for the DWD. It came from the Greek word *xeri*, meaning dry. Because the *x* is pronounced like a *z*, some people call it *zero*-scaping and think of it as minimalist landscaping, i.e., rocks and gravel and cactus. In fact, nothing could be further from the truth.

Don't think of gravel as those boring gray pebbles they dump on country roads. In Sun City, Arizona, it's a colorful landscaping statement. The statement is, "I'm retired, and I've mowed my last lawn!"

This homeowner in the Southwest installed Astroturf in his front yard. Great for conserving water and, as an added bonus, he never has to mow. All he needs now is Astrohedge!

Landscaping Revolutionary: Benny J. Simpson (1928–1996)

Benny was many things to many people: a research scientist, a horticultural pioneer, an explorer, a mentor . . . and a worrier. What Benny worried about most was droughts. He remembered the terrible droughts that had devastated his native Texas back in the 1950s—he knew they came in cycles, every twenty years or so—and that was the underlying reason why he devoted over a quarter of a century to preaching the gospel of native plants.

Benny called himself a "plant hunter," and his countless forays into the wilds of Texas in search of natives were legendary. He was primarily interested in finding plants that could be developed for the commercial nursery trade, and over the years he found many. Among them are desert willow, a mountain sage called Mount Emory, and cenizos (*Leucophyllum* species). Shortly after Benny's death, *Dallas Morning News* writer Bryan Wooley recalled the time he'd accompanied Benny out to the Big Bend desert. "I think of Benny every time I see a cenizo bush. Benny taught me to regard that

humble shrub, which I had known all my life, in a new way. His joy made me see how beautiful it is."

"You didn't go far in native plants until someone told you to talk to Benny," says Jill Nokes, Austin landscape designer and author. "He influenced a whole generation of horticulturists." Sally and I depended heavily on him when we wrote our first book, *Native Texas Plants: Landscaping Region by Region*. In the dedication, we wrote, "It would take another whole book to relate how grateful we are for his wise counsel, amazing knowledge, and infinite patience, without which this book simply would not have been possible." In truth, much of Benny lives in these pages, as well.

Benny was himself an author; he wrote numerous

articles on native plants for various gardening magazines, and his book, *A Field Guide to Texas Trees*, which came out in 1990, is recognized as *the* standard reference on the subject. A book on native shrubs was nearing completion at the time of his death. Tragically, all his notes and range maps have been lost.

In 1982, Benny helped found the Native Plant Society of Texas, which today has thirty-one chapters and over seventeen hundred members. He hosted every annual meeting of the organization up until the year before his death, and members recall fondly not only his wit, but his uncanny ability to get speakers on and off on schedule, without ruffling any feathers.

At his memorial service, words of praise came from such luminaries as Lady Bird Johnson and Vice President Al Gore. But mostly it was a gathering of friends, former students, and colleagues who shared fond and sometimes humorous memories of this very special person. As Bryan Wooley noted, "Benny was a rare one."

The definition of xeriscaping, "water conservation through creative landscaping," was initially applied to low-rainfall regions. But today, the term applies equally well all over the country, even in high-rainfall areas where they can still have water problems. In other words, *xeriscaping simply means using plant materials that can exist on whatever rainfall the area gets naturally*. That means you can have a xeriscape in Louisiana, where they get some sixty inches (150 cm) of rain annually, or in Tucson, with just eight inches (20 cm) annually.

New concepts usually don't take hold overnight (there is still an active Flat Earth Society out there), but every now and again a good and sensible idea *does* meet with success. Today, water departments all over the

The Denver Water Department led the way in recognizing the demands home landscapes put on a city's water supply. Here, where xeriscaping was born, a demonstration garden, featuring local native flora, shows homeowners that beauty can be achieved with a fraction of the water they now use for conventional landscapes.

The typical American landscape is alive and well in Alaska. When we arrived there for my niece's wedding, they were having a drought. The temperatures were in the eighties and people were reeling in the streets—and watering their traditional American landscapes every night.

country are promoting xeriscaping, and are mailing out millions of bill-stuffers urging customers to practice the basic principles of water-saving landscaping.

The following sensible watering tips combine the basic Xeriscape principles advocated by the Denver Water Department and suggestions my wife, Sally, gives to her landscape design customers:

1. Get rid of all or a significant portion of your conventional turf grass area. Remember, the lawn is a water guzzler. Consider alternatives such as native ground covers or grasses. Or, decks or patios.
2. Use plants that are native to your immediate area (within fifty to one hundred miles, or 80 to 161 km), or noninvasive exotics that are well suited to your growing conditions.

3. Always water in the coolest parts of the day, preferably after sundown.
4. Water in two short cycles instead of one long one to reduce runoff. Better yet, use a drip irrigation or bubbler system; these are far more efficient.
5. Water deeply. When the water gets down to a depth of four to six inches (10 to 15 cm), the roots are encouraged to grow down deeper, where it stays moist longer.
6. Aerate the soil for better water penetration.
7. Use mulches, such as bark chips and straw or decomposed granite, around trees and shrubs. They keep the roots cool and reduce evaporation by as much as 70 percent.
8. Check your irrigation system for leaks. Even a teeny one can waste incredible amounts of water.

9. Separate plants according to their water needs; low-water plants all together and higher-water plants in another place. Take advantage of existing water in the landscape, such as a creek, pond, or recycling fountain, or even the extra moisture gained where rain runs off your roof or patio.

Since its introduction, Xeriscape garden clubs have sprung up around the country, and a National Xeriscape Council was formed to further promote this water-wise concept. By 1990, there were active educational programs in more than sixty cities in forty-two states, and three foreign countries. In addition, *The Xeriscape Color Guide* was recently published by the Denver Water Department, giving gardeners and landscape designers a valuable tool in planning water-wise gardens with an evolving, year-round harmony of colors. And, I'm reliably informed, some water-conscious folks even hold Xeriscapic garden parties, which they advertise as "X-Rated"! Cute.

Here's a good example of just how drought-tolerant native plants can be: this site in Austin, Texas, used to be a Whole Foods Market. In March, they moved on to bigger and better quarters, leaving this corner landscape (about 90 percent native) untended and unwatered throughout a very hot and dry summer. I shot this photo in late September. It's still green and you can see blooms. Of course, it could use a little pruning, but otherwise it's healthy and attractive. Try this with a conventional landscape.

Same state, same city, same drought, but now we're looking at a Xeriscape composed of native fireweed and elderberry. Does this look like a drought to you?

Chapter 3

THERE'S GOTTA BE A BETTER WAY!

"Your lawn looks great," she said. "Great? This belongs in a magazine. I've never seen a puttin' green look this good. I deserve garden of the month." "It's incredible. How many times a week do you mow?" "Three or four."

John Grisham
The Firm

Having read this far, you are no doubt already teetering on the edge of enlistment in the landscaping revolution. You've been awed by my lucid arguments against the traditional American landscape, you are impressed by the unassailable logic of going more native and natural, and you are feeling faint stirrings of impatience—you want to rip out your lawn and get on with it.

But get on with what exactly? At this point, you may still be harboring some fairly basic questions as to what being a landscape revolutionary really entails. Are there dues? Monthly meetings? Will you have to march in demonstrations?

In fact, it couldn't be easier. All it takes to be a part of the landscaping revolution is to use those plants that can survive without your constantly fussing over them.

And those plants are, by and large, native plants.

What a Native Plant Is . . . and Isn't

All plants have native ancestry. Even all that hybridized flora at your nursery came from plants that once thrived in the wilds of their original homes . . . Asia, Africa, wherever. Some, such as tea roses, have been so genetically altered and weakened by horticulturists that they wouldn't have a prayer of surviving on their own. Other nursery plants have been selected for color or fragrance but have *not* been hybridized by people, and so still retain their genetic heritage. Take them back to where they came from, plant them in the wild, and they'd probably do OK. But put them in the ground where you live and that may not be the case. Back where they came from, they may have gotten more—or less— rainfall than they're finding in your yard. There, the winters may have been colder, the summers hotter, the springs earlier. There,

they had built-in defenses against local diseases and pests. Here, in your yard, they're in alien surroundings and need a lot of help. These are the plants that constitute the bulk of landscape stock.

There are other imports that find conditions here hospitable; conditions that are similar to their native conditions, and they do very well. They naturalize in their new homes—that is, they escape the confines of a garden and grow successfully in the wild. Some naturalized plants—lilacs, peonies, bearded irises, crape myrtles, and antique roses—are well behaved and, in the right conditions, can be good additions to a home's landscape. Trouble is, hundreds of these naturalized plants are aggressive and, lacking the natural controls they had back home, they run amok in their new surroundings and create environmental problems. These are invasives, and we'll talk more about them in Chapter 5.

Plants that are native to your area, then, have three main distinguishing characteristics:

- They arrived in floods, in the fur of migrating mammals, in bird or animal droppings, or wafted on the wind.
- They evolved over a very long period of time so as to be able to thrive in their specific local conditions. Some North American natives have been in their areas for millions of years, some since the last ice age, and all certainly since before European settlers came to these shores.
- They've never been genetically tampered with by us. Some plants we think of as native don't qualify because of this very point. Take corn. True native corn is no longer around; thousands of years ago people genetically improved it for their agricultural needs.

Put simply, the term *native* is all about *location and genetic purity*.

Another important point to understand: plants are native to vegetational regions and not states or other artificially concocted areas. In 1988 Sally and I wrote *Native Texas Plants: Landscaping Region by Region*. And while the 399 plants we profiled in the book were indeed native to the Lone Star State, none was native to the *whole* state; in the book we described ten distinct vegetational zones within Texas, and profiled the specific plants that were indigenous to each of those zones. We tried to make it crystal clear that a plant indigenous to arid west Texas, for example, could not be used along the much wetter Gulf Coast.

Moreover, a plant that is native to your general area is really native to a specific habitat within your area. For example, American sycamore *Platanus occidentalis* may be native to your city, but only in creek bottoms, not on rocky hilltops. If you live on a rocky hill, American sycamore is not suitable for your yard. Unless you grossly overwater everything else, it will be damaged by anthracnose, defoliate in late summer, and in general look pathetic instead of majestic.

By the way, the terms *native* and *indigenous* are synonymous, as any standard dictionary and thesaurus will confirm. But from time to time I've met people who think that, botanically, the words have slightly different meanings. They use native in a general sense

Two "Texas natives." Yet clearly, their environments are very different. When found in the wild, spider lily *Hymenocallis liriosme* is going to be in or very near water—in eastern Texas. Now look at the cenizo *Leucophyllum candidum*. It's in hotter and more arid parts of the state and grows happily in caliche, sand, and limestone. You wouldn't want both plants in the same garden. By the way, spider lily is also native in parts of Oklahoma, Louisiana, and Mississippi, while cenizo is native down into Mexico. You see what I mean about state lines being pretty much meaningless when you are defining what is a native.

and indigenous to more precisely pinpoint a locale—as in, this plant is native to the southeast and indigenous to wetlands, marshes, and bogs. The botanical authorities I've consulted dismiss this approach and maintain that the words can be used interchangeably, which is what I do throughout this book.

But because indigenous is one of those five-dollar words and used far less commonly, it is often *mis*used—sometimes with interesting consequences. A few years back I saw a TV commercial for Home Depot inviting people to shop their stock of "indigenous plants." I was pleasantly surprised, to say the least. If this national chain was indeed carrying indigenous plants, it was a big step forward for the landscaping revolution. So I called three of the nearest locations to find out exactly *which* indigenous plants they carried.

The salespeople in the gardening sections didn't have a clue what I was talking about. Clearly, they didn't know what indigenous meant, so I explained. "Oh, sure," one of them responded cheerily, "we carry natives. We have crape myrtles!" Well, yes, crape myrtles *are* natives—to China!

I finally called the company's advertising department in Atlanta and spoke to a customer service representative who informed me that what they'd meant by indigenous was "plants that are *grown* locally." In other words, if they were growing tulips and marigolds at or near the store, they considered these plants to be "indigenous."

When I told her what the word really meant, the representative seemed grateful for the information, and I haven't seen the commercial since. One more blow for truth in advertising . . . and botany!

Provenance Is Not a City in Rhode Island

Now that you know what a native plant is, you're well on your way to gardening suc-

cess. All you have to do is find out which species are native where you live, stick 'em in the ground, and then wait for the inevitable call from a photographer wanting to immortalize your efforts on the cover of *Fine Gardening*.

Right?

Well, no . . . this is not always the case.

You see, while getting the species right is a big part of successful gardening, it won't do you much good if you don't get the *provenance* right as well.

Provenance means "place of origin." Botanically, it means where a plant evolved. And *where* it evolved determines its "genotype," i.e., its genetic composition.

As we noted, a specific plant can be native to a number of places—not just within one vegetational zone, but in very diverse sections of the country. When plants do evolve in just one specific spot, they are called *endemics*—they exist in that one spot and nowhere else.

So, when we talk about the provenance of a specific plant, we are not talking about the species as a whole, we're talking about the specific genotype of a specific plant *within* that species—the one you see in the nursery and may be thinking of buying for your yard. *One with a local provenance will be genetically better suited to your local growing conditions than one that is indigenous to another part of the country with very different growing conditions*. It's the provenance of a plant that truly determines whether or not it's native or indigenous to your region.

Let's use butterflyweed *Asclepias tuberosa* as an example. Native in sandhills, flatwoods, post oak woods, meadows, and pinelands throughout the eastern two-thirds of the U.S., from eastern South Dakota down into Florida, this brilliant orange-colored plant has a very long taproot, making it extremely drought tolerant and long-lived. Even so, butterflyweeds from our northern states would succumb to the hotter summers of the Deep South, while butterflyweeds

Would Caesar Understand?

One more bit of information to make you a well-informed landscape revolutionary. And it's about something that really scares the dickens out of some gardeners—needlessly. I'm referring to Latin names.

Plants have been given those double Latin names ever since Swedish botanist Carolus Linnaeus (sounds like a plant himself, doesn't he?) came up with the system back in 1753. The first name signifies the genus; the second signifies the species. Although these names may sometimes look impossible to get your tongue around, they still provide us with the most precise method of identification. Common names can vary depending on locality, but the Latin names remain the same universally. So, when a botanist from Lima, Ohio, meets one from Lima, Peru, they can still talk shop using Latin names.

This system also means that you are far more likely to get exactly the plant you want. If your landscape designer calls for *Salvia greggii* and you buy *Salvia farinacea*, you will wind up with a blue-flowered perennial instead of the red-flowered shrub that was intended.

Latin names may change from time to time because botanists are still reclassifying and even still discovering plants. These botanists fall into two categories: the lumpers and the splitters, and sometimes they decide that two plants that were considered to be of different species are really the same after all, or that a certain species is, in reality, two different ones. Three years or so down the road they'll reverse themselves. In our own books, Sally and I have found that the Latin names were changed on a number of plants from one printing to the next. This drives garden writers crazy!

And please, don't sweat the pronunciations. If you dissect them phonetically, they really aren't as hard as they may first appear. Besides, what with all our regional accents, almost nobody pronounces them the same, anyway. Including the pros.

Using Latin names is really the best way to get what you want. Both of these plants are of the genus *Salvia*, but if you don't add the species, *S. greggii*, a red perennial, you could wind up with *S. farinacea*, a blue-flowered shrub. Sally tells me that landscape designers can get pretty testy when this happens.

The butterflyweed on the left is from Texas, and the one on the right is from Illinois. They are of the same genus and species, *Asclepias tuberosa*, yet have very different genetic makeups. They really don't like each other's native habitats.

indigenous to Georgia or Alabama would find Minnesota winters intolerable.

Then there's the live oak *Quercus virginiana*. This tree is native from the southern Atlantic coast to central Texas and Oklahoma. Now, if you happen to live within that geographical range, you might figure any old live oak will do well in your landscape. But what if you live in, say, Dallas, and your nursery purchased its live oaks from some out-of-state grower. Well, if there's a repeat of the notorious winter of 1983–84—when north-central Texas became a deep freeze—your live oak could be in big trouble.

Back then, half the live oaks popped their barks and died—the half that had come from growers in southern Louisiana. The half that came through pretty much unscathed were the indigenous ones from local growers. These were genetically suited to the kind of extreme winters that periodically hit that part of the state.

If you live in Connecticut, you might want to add native snowberry *Symphoricarpos albus* to your landscape. This handsome, shady ground cover, with its clusters of white berries in fall and winter, is native in your locale, but it's also native in a giant horseshoe-shaped range that stretches from southern California (where it is known as canyon snowberry) up to Alaska, then across to Quebec and on down to Virginia!

If the snowberry you buy is from a mail-order catalog out of, say, Oregon or one your local nursery bought from a grower in California, it might not do well for you if you live in Connecticut.

Life would be a lot easier for us if plants of the same species but very different provenances *looked* different. Then a live oak, for example, from Georgia would be somehow visually set apart from one in Texas. No such luck; members of the same species usually look pretty much the same, no matter where they originated. Of course, botanists realize that these plants are different, and they divide them into varieties—in the case of live oaks, into coastal live oaks and escarpment live oaks. But it's a very rare nursery that will label their stock this definitively.

You need to know, too, that provenance affects more than winter hardiness; drought and summer hardiness are also important considerations. Possumhaw *Ilex decidua* is a gorgeous ornamental tree that is native from Virginia and Illinois on down to the Gulf of Mexico. And it's a beaut: the female is ablaze with red berries from November through March, when new leaves appear.

But if you live in Tulsa and your nursery carries possumhaws that are native to the Carolinas, where the rainfall averages up to thirty inches (76 cm) more per year than it does in possumhaw's western range, these trees aren't going to be happy in your yard this summer. They will be drought stressed and vulnerable to insects and diseases.

Both the netleaf hackberry *Celtis reticulata*, a.k.a. *palo blanco* or *acibuche* and the popular evergreen shrub jojoba or goatnut *Simmondsia chinesis* are native from the Sonoran Desert of Mexico on over to southern California. But if you live in San Diego and your nursery purchased these two natives from a grower in Phoenix, Arizona, their provenance would not be the coastal chaparral of San Diego County, but the Sonoran Desert. And even though San Diego and Phoenix may be similar in some respects, they do not share the exact same growing conditions. Both the San Diego hackberry and jojoba will be used to a much more humid climate and milder summers and will not thrive in Phoenix.

Big bluestem *Andropogon gerardi*, also known as turkeyfoot, is the most important grass in the tallgrass prairies. It has a very wide native range, from the Gulf of Mexico up into southern Canada, and from Florida to New Mexico. It can grow in moist areas out in West Texas, on hillsides in Wisconsin, and in meadows in New York State. But if you think a big bluestem adapted to the high humidity around Baton Rouge, Louisiana, is going to do well in the high aridity of Albuquerque, think again.

With annuals, provenance isn't such a big deal. But with longer-lived plants—especially trees—that affect large parts of your landscape, it's important to choose a specimen that will withstand all of the vagaries that the weather might produce. It needs to be from the same latitude, from the same altitude, the

Snowberry **Symphoricarpos albus** has an amazingly large native range, going from southern California to Alaska, then over to Quebec and down to Virginia. Talk about a variety of growing conditions!

same distance from the moderating influence of the ocean, and the same distance from any mountains that might affect rainfall patterns. It must also have the same kind of soil porosity, with the same range of alkalinity or acidity. Otherwise, a winter storm or drought will damage it.

Bottom line: Before you purchase your native, don't check just the species, check out the provenance as well. If you buy one whose provenance is within one hundred miles of where you live, it ought to do well. And if the people at your nursery don't know, and can't

find out, you run the risk of buying and planting something that may be beautiful and even appropriate for local wildlife, but it may not be any more of a sure thing than an exotic plant.

Landscape Styles

One of the criticisms of native plants that Sally and I have come across is that they limit one's creative expression. The idea being, I guess, that if you use natives, you have to

Landscaping Revolutionary: Lorrie Otto

He arrived early one morning without prior notice. He had been sent by the village officials of Bayside, Wisconsin, and his mission was simple—to mow down Lorrie Otto's fern garden. It was, to

their eyes, a weed patch, and had to go in order to preserve the dignity and order of the small community. When he left, nothing remained but the stubble and debris of her once healthy and beautiful landscape.

Lorrie was infuriated by her community's high-handed arrogance, and she confronted the village officials head-on. "Natural landscaping is a public good," she pointed out, "not a health hazard." She was heard, and her arguments were unassailable. In the end, the village paid her damages. Lorrie had chalked up her first victory against ignorance and for our environment. It would not be her last.

Her friend Rochelle Whiteman calls Lorrie "a gentle creative force, sensitive to Nature's design." *Newsweek* magazine calls her the "high priestess" of the Natural Landscaping Movement, *National Wildlife* refers to Lorrie as "the God-mother" of natural landscaping, and Craig Tufts, of the National Wildlife Federation, calls Lorrie the "heart and soul of the movement." The year 1998 was a big one for Lorrie: she was featured on Tom Brokaw's NBC *Nightly News* and was the recipient of a Connie, the National Wildlife Federation's coveted Conservation Achievement Award.

She is a tireless evangelist, preaching that con-

have a wild and natural look around your house. While this is a look we personally like a lot, we've seen natives used in a wide variety of landscaping plans. Natives are nothing if not versatile. And to prove it, Sally once designed a very formal garden using nothing but natives—parterres, symmetrical layout, the works. It was a miniature garden of Versailles.

We've also seen natives used in traditional landscapes, with native buffalograss lawns, and a range of colorful native shrubs and flowers. In other words, the kind of landscape that would not arouse the hackles of even your most conservative neighbors.

When you start out using natives, you may very well want to start with a more conventional look. Well and good. You'll still reap the benefits of lower maintenance and water use.

But the day may well come when you are ready to take the big step of moving away from the conventional landscape look completely and going a little more natural—that is, copying in some measure the look Mother Nature had in mind.

servation begins at home, in one's own front and backyards. She takes a positive stance, viewing those vast expanses of urban and suburban development not so much as a blight, but as an environmental opportunity. "If suburbia were landscaped with meadows, prairies, thickets, or forests, or combinations of these," she says, "then the water would sparkle, fish would be good to eat again, birds would sing, and human spirits would rise."

A founding board member of the Wisconsin chapter of the Nature Conservancy, and a member of the Citizens Natural Resources Association, Lorrie was active in the successful effort to ban ddt from Wisconsin—it was the first state to do so. Later, when Wisconsin senator Gaylord Nelson sponsored a federal law to ban ddt throughout the United States, he quoted Lorrie Otto in Senate hearings on the proposed ban. Lorrie's common sense was being heard across the country.

Lorrie continues to speak before gardening and environmental groups, wherever and whenever she sees a chance to convert people into natural landscapers. In the 1980s, she formed the Wild Ones Natural Landscapers, Ltd., an educational organization dedicated to preserving native plants by encouraging natural landscapes. The organization now has chapters in eleven states.

In 1994, Lorrie spoke at a weed ordinance workshop attended by fifty municipal officials who wanted to learn how to use natural landscaping in their communities. Imagine how Lorrie felt. Where once she and city officials went toe-to-toe in court, today they work side by side. And at a recent banquet in her honor, Bayside presented Lorrie with a proclamation declaring the community's pride in its most famous resident and her very special garden.

Here, you have two options, *natural* and *naturalistic*. Unlike *native* and *indigenous*, these words are not synonymous.

The Natural Landscape

In a **natural landscape**, you are using only those plants that are native to your area. It's a purist thing, and admittedly, it's not for everyone. If you're creating a native garden from scratch on the land*scraped* property the builder left for you, or you're converting from a conventional landscape, then going 100 percent indigenous can be a bit of a challenge. It's doable, and the end result is worthwhile, but it may be a tad more work than you want to undertake. Especially since, depending on where you live, it can be a problem finding enough indigenous plant materials—seeds, saplings, cuttings, and so on.

A natural landscape is a copy of what Mother Nature did in the first place. Or, in the case of building on an unspoiled piece of land, it is exactly what the old girl had in mind (see Chapter 11). In either case, it is a functioning ecosystem that supports wildlife and is virtually self-sustaining. A little cosmetic pruning, weeding out an uninvited alien that some bird or squirrel contributed, and maybe a little watering for aesthetic purposes during a particularly dry spell, and that's about it.

The Naturalistic Landscape

The **naturalistic landscape** is far more relaxed than a traditional landscape, but not as purist as a natural one. Severe pruning of trees and shrubs is rejected in favor of softer, more natural shapes. There is no need to go totally indigenous here. Noninvasive alien plants that are well adapted to your area are used, either completely or in combination with indigenous plants. And human touches, such as stone paths, water features, or seating areas are often added.

This landscape looks pretty much like all the others up and down the street, with one big exception: virtually everything you see here is native to the area. This home belongs to Connie and Glenn Suhrens in Garland, Texas.

Whether it has been re-created or preserved, the natural landscape copies the natural world designed by Mother Nature. Totally indigenous, it is extremely low maintenance. And it provides sanctuary for wildlife, giving back to the critters some of the natural habitats we've taken away through development and lumbering. This is the home of Mary and Dick Stanley in Dellwood, Minnesota.

The naturalistic landscape may be composed of well-adapted non-natives, or a mixture of natives and non-natives, as shown here. This was our home in Dallas. The plants were 70 percent indigenous, with the rest coming from other parts of Texas, the South, and even a few foreigners from Asia and Europe. The style is relaxed and colorful, with an ever-changing palette of colors and textures throughout the year.

Myths and Misconceptions

A nursery owner actually told me that the reason he didn't carry any native plants was "because if I did, I'd soon be out of business."

His reasoning was based on the fact—acknowledged even by non-native gardeners—that native plants are a very hearty lot. They thrive on minimum watering, easily handle the occasional unexpected freeze or drought, and, when used in a natural setting with a diversity of other compatible natives, have no need for pesticides.

To understand his position, you first have to know that a large part of his business is replacements—selling *more* non-native plants to replace the ones that didn't survive. If everyone started using rugged, well-adapted natives, he reasoned, the very foundation of his business would crumble.

While his attitude may make you smile, understand that he is not unique. Myths and misconceptions abound when the subject of native plants arises—ranging from the idea that they are "bullet-proof" to the bizarre notion, actually voiced by a well-known garden writer, that to be successful with natives "one has to live like a bear in the wilderness."

Thinking that natives are bulletproof, homeowners buy one or two for their otherwise conventional landscapes, and then continue to water for the benefit of the exotics. Guess what happens! The natives drown, and the homeowners are disillusioned and say, "Hah! Natives aren't so tough after all!"

Native plants can survive on rainfall alone. How do you think they got along all those millennia before we invented irrigation systems? In a garden setting, a little supplemental watering is fine, just to keep them looking their best. But *over*watering is, in most cases, a death sentence. And that, by the way, applies to standard nursery stock as well. Overwatering kills off more of them than any other cause.

So, now that you know these basic facts about natives, let's move on to the native plant palettes that make the landscaping revolution possible.

Chapter 4

THE NATIVES ARE FRIENDLY

"It is not good try-
ing to force plants
to adopt a way of
life they don't like;
they just won't have
it unless you are rich
enough to undertake
excavations the size of
a quarry."

**Vita Sackville-West
British Gardening Author**

Gardeners can be divided into two groups. The first belongs to the Evel Kneivel school of gardening. They see gardening as an eternal challenge—an us versus Mother Nature situation, where the environment must be overpowered and bent to one's will. These are the people who insist on growing azaleas in alkaline soil, banana trees in zone 8, and turf grass in areas with a mere eight to twelve inches (20 to 30 cm) of annual rainfall. Into this group I also lump bungie jumpers, people who build Spanish galleons inside aspirin bottles, and liberals running for office in Orange County.

The second category is the one Sally and I belong to. We consistently opt for the path of least resistance—the easiest way possible. Getting a plant to not only stay alive, but actually thrive, is an achievement that strikes us as being only slightly less intimidating than pulling off an orbital docking maneuver. Forget having green thumbs; ours range from beige to black!

Little wonder then that we gravitate toward native plants the way iron filings gravitate toward magnets. And little wonder that the essence of the landscaping revolution is the appreciation and use of these natives.

Native Lawn Alternatives

Fortunately, no matter where in the country we live, we have a vast palette of native plants to meet our landscaping needs. And that includes lawn grasses! The thing is, we revolutionaries understood from the very beginning that we were not going to attract certain people to this movement if they thought for one moment that they'd have to give up their lawns. Sure, they wanted to be environmentally correct, of course they wanted to save water, and yes, they weren't adverse to reducing their landscaping workload. But lawns there would have to be!

And so new varieties of turf grass were developed to conserve water. In 1988, the

This lawn is 'Prairie' buffalograss. It was watered just once all summer, yet look how green it is. The bermudagrass lawn on the left was watered thirty-three times, and it still looks stressed. In the winter, even when dormant, the buffalograss lawn is attractive, with a soft, golden hue, while the bermudagrass looks gray and dead.

USDA introduced a new zoysia grass for that purpose, and later announced blends of zoysia and fescue that offer homeowners the added bonus of staying green all year.

But the big news was buffalograss *Buchloe dactyloides*. Native throughout the Great Plains, from Minnesota to Montana and as far south as Peru—wherever conditions aren't too moist, too shady, or too sandy—it evolved through many centuries of both cyclic and prolonged dry spells so that it requires a fraction of the water required by even the best of the non-natives—only an inch and a half (4 cm) of rainfall a month to stay green (actually a pretty blueish green, although there are variations), where bermudagrass needs three to four inches (8 to 10 cm), and St. Augustine and tall fescue require five to six inches (13 to 15 cm).

Needless to say, when it was tried as a lawn grass, it was quickly hailed as an environmental breakthrough in many quarters. Buffalograss is also so slow growing that mowing becomes a once to four times a summer chore.

It's also tough, and can take a lot of foot traffic. In the athletic department, a soccer field has been sodded with it and the buffalograss turf has held up very well. It covers quickly, needs less fertilizer, and outlives conventional turf grasses. It forms a dense sod that keeps weeds from getting a root in edgewise; pure stands in the wild are not uncommon. In addition, it stays out of flower beds; its roots are not at all invasive.

If you're in a part of the country where buffalograss makes sense, here are a few tips on getting it established:

- It's fairly easy to find these days. Nurseries are now carrying varieties in seed, plugs, and sods.
- Bed preparation is needed for all three forms. If your soil has been compacted, deep till to a depth of eighteen to twenty-four inches (45 to 60 cm) to promote deep root growth. Otherwise, working

the soil to a normal gardenlike consistency will suffice.
- Get rid of all other vegetation in the planting area.

The biggest problem some homeowners have with buffalograss is when a neighbor's turf grass invades and takes over. But this happens only when the buffalograss homeowner forgets why it was installed in the first place, and *overwaters* it.

At first, standard-issue buffalograss was used—the same kind that had grown abundantly throughout the Great Plains. By the turn of the century, after decades of overgrazing by sheep and cattle, buffalograss had virtually disappeared, and was replaced by imported European and African grasses that were judged to be better adapted for livestock. Soon, numerous cultivars such as 'Comanche,' 'Texoka,' 'Plains,' and 'Top Gun' were introduced, offering variations in color, foliage, density, length of dormancy, and height. Some homeowners preferred to leave these grasses unmowed, and lawns twelve to sixteen inches (30 to 40 cm) tall graced many yards, undulating in the breezes and presenting a nostalgic glimpse of what had once carpeted our prairies from horizon to horizon.

But we had become accustomed to the perfections of golf-course-style lawns—thicker thatches and softer textures—and so, by the 1990s, new varieties of buffalograss were on the market, designed to look even more lawnlike. Two of the most popular—'Prairie,' developed at Texas A&M by Dr. Milt Engelke, and '609,' created by Dr. Terry Riordan at the University of Nebraska—grew to a maximum height of eight to ten inches (20 to 25 cm). Another variety, 'Stampede,' sold in sod, grows to just four inches (10 cm). Only those who crave the crew-cut look have to continue mowing. These new varieties also have a softer, more lawnlike texture that invites bare feet.

Meanwhile, development goes on with other native grasses such as the even more drought-tolerant blue grama *Bouteloua gracilis* and the heat-tolerant Texas bluegrass *Poa arachnifera*, which is being hybridized with Kentucky bluegrass *Poa pratensis*.

But despite the successes of these grasses, there was a growing sentiment in many quarters that the days of the lawn-centered landscape were numbered. Around the country, *living* alternatives to gravel and concrete are being used successfully.

Moss   Don't laugh. If you live where it's humid—from Canada down through Dixie—and you have lots of shade, you can have a velvety soft, low-upkeep moss lawn.

Several years ago, Sally and I visited Louise "Weezie" Smith in Birmingham, Alabama. Weezie is known throughout the South for her wonderful native landscape, and garden magazine photographers are a common sight on her five-acre property. What especially struck us was the moss lawn that graced the north side of her home.

"It used to be ordinary turf grass, and the children used to play on it," she told us.

"But when they grew up and moved away, I decided I didn't want to spend all that time mowing and all, so I just ignored it." Before very long, Weezie was surprised to see that her turf grass had been taken over by moss, which is abundant on her property.

"My first reaction was that I'd have to get rid of it and restore the lawn—but then I saw how attractive it was and decided to leave it alone." In fact, that's exactly what she has done over the past years; the moss lawn is remarkably low maintenance. It needs no seeding, no pesticides, and no watering. When we were visiting, Birmingham was having a drought, with temperatures reaching 100 degrees, but Weezie's moss lawn looked great.

If you think a moss lawn might make sense for you, but you can't find any moss on your property, Weezie has a suggestion: get some from a neighbor or in the woods, put it in a blender with buttermilk (for acidity and as a carrier), give it a few seconds at puree, and then just spread it around with a putty knife or squeegee, and mist it frequently to get it off and running.

Our friend Lorine Gibson, in Dallas, recommends adding a bit of manure to the blend, but in that case you'd have to throw out the blender. But in most cases, moss needn't be recruited—it volunteers.

Ground Covers   Do you struggle like crazy trying to grow grass in shady areas, and fail anyway? Native ground covers make a lot more sense, and there are lots of them. There are two schools of thought on ground covers. The first is the traditional view that a ground cover should be evergreen, low to the ground (under eight to nine inches [20 to 23 cm] high), and ought to be used as a monoculture, that is, never planted in company with other plants. Because it is used as a lawn substitute—especially where shade trees make growing turf grass difficult if not impossible—many believe the ground cover ought to look as lawnlike as possible.

In Lubbock, Texas, Reverend Davis Price puts his kids' training wheels on his mower to keep his buffalograss lawn at a six-inch (15-cm) height, giving it a wonderfully shaggy texture.

In many parts of the country, from Canada down into Dixie, moss grows profusely and can be an excellent alternative to conventional turf grasses. This moss lawn is in Birmingham, Alabama, and looks lush and healthy, even though this picture was taken during a long and hot dry spell.

The other school is from the European and Japanese gardening traditions, and it is much more flexible. There, numerous plants are considered to be ground covers that many American gardeners would reject out of hand—deciduous plants, ferns, flowers, shrubs, and vines—and mixing a number of genera and species of varying heights, textures, and colors is not only considered OK but preferable. Personally, I think it's a lot more interesting and attractive to combine several varieties: woodland flowers, ferns, low-growing leafy shrubs . . . all interacting as they do in nature. And here's a secret: it's not only prettier, it's healthier. Diversity of species is one of Mother Nature's best tricks for combating disease and infestations of garden pests.

Both approaches are valid, so we'll look at some of the best native ground covers from around the country—for the shade and for sunny areas—and leave the execution of your landscape to your own tastes and circumstances.

Many nurseries now carry a good selection of native ground covers, but if yours doesn't, and you don't have a native nursery nearby, you might consider a plant rescue. If you see construction starting up in a natural area—either virgin or recovering—get permission from the owners, and then dig up the ground covers you like for transplanting in your garden. (In fact, rescue as many as you can and give the extras to friends or your neighborhood school or civic center.)

But before you replant them around your home, take a look at the home environment the ground covers are currently growing in. If they're used to a stable woodland setting, for example, where the soil is spongy underfoot and rich in natural nutrients, will they find similar conditions in your garden? In the woodland, the soil is well aerated by

This home in Northampton, Massachusetts, displays a variety of ferns, including hayscented fern, ostrich fern, and sensitive fern. Also in this landscape are mayapple, witch hazel, American ginger, flowering dogwood, wavy-leaved aster, white snakeroot, crested iris, and native geranium. The design was by landscape architect Ruth Parnall of Conway.

earthworms and covered with a loose mulch of decomposing leaves. On a typical forest floor there are three years of fallen leaves visible at all times. The top one to two inches (2.5 to 5 cm) are recognizably dead leaves, while beneath that is an inch of half-decomposed leaves, and then an inch or more of compost. Below that, the compost is mixed with the soil.

If your existing landscape is typical, it is not yet a good site for woodland ground covers. Your soil is probably compacted from years of mowing, walking, and watering. Chemicals have killed off the microorganisms and earthworms that are necessary for healthy soil. And, because leaves and mowed grass have been raked, bagged, and carted off—usually to the landfill—there is no natural mulch.

So, before you bring ground covers into your landscape, you'll need to return organic matter to the soil and perhaps use some compost starter. Let's look at some of the ground covers you may want to adopt. We'll give you the Latin and common names, the native range (where it grows naturally), and a few other tidbits of useful information. As with all the other plant categories we'll sample in these pages, this is just a small and random sampling from the many hundreds of possibilities from all around the country.

For example, **ferns** are wonderful ground covers in moist, shady spots all over the country except for the hot, dry Southwest. Refer to regional plant guides or local native plant or wildflower societies for lists of suitable ferns that are native to your area.

1. *Antennaria plantaginifolia*, **pussytoes. Dry woodlands, eastern North America.** Ideal for lightly shaded, dry landscapes, it grows in two-inch-high (5-cm) mats. In the early spring, expect to see tiny clusters of fuzzy white blossoms the shape and size of pussy's toes. The female flowers are pinkish. Pussytoes delivers a smooth show of silver green leaves for all but two weeks out of the year. *Other species of pussytoes, all desirable, can be found in various parts of the country.* Although most have silvery leaves, some have leaves that are green edged with silver, and some have leaves that are all green. Plains pussytoes *Antennaria parvifolia* is native to dry shortgrass prairies in Manitoba, British Columbia (where the species is better known as *Antennaria aprica*), western Minnesota, eastern Washington, and through the Dakotas to northwestern Oklahoma, northern Arizona, and Nevada. That's some range! But then, it seems that the whole pussytoes family has far-reaching native ranges. Ladies' tobacco *A. parlinii* is native from Maine down to Alabama and over into Kansas, Nebraska, eastern Texas and Oklahoma, and up to Minnesota. Field pussytoes *A. neglecta* grows in moist remnant prairies from Canada to Pennsylvania, Ohio, Oklahoma, Colorado, and Montana.

Pussytoes *Antennaria plantaginifolia*

2. *Asarum canadense*, **wild ginger. Rich woods in zones 3 to 7 of eastern North America.** The valentine-shaped leaves, three to six inches (8 to 15 cm) across, make a rich texture that looks great in either large or small areas. Height is about six inches (15 cm), and health and vigor are a comfort to amateur gardeners. Wild ginger greens up in early spring and doesn't go dormant until a killing frost. Although it can form a dense ground cover by itself, it can also be used as a base for wild ferns and woodland flowers. In winter, let it be mulched by fallen leaves from the trees that shade it.

3. *Baccharis pilularis*, **coyote brush. Coastal bluffs and oak woodlands, from Mexico north to Oregon.** A sunny ground cover with very good drought tolerance, the warm-green evergreen leaves have a fine texture that gives coyote brush high marks for ornamental value. This low-growing shrub forms masses two and a half feet by five feet (80 cm by 150 cm), sometimes larger. With age, it will develop gentle mounds and waves.

4. *Calyptocarpus vialis*, **horseherb. Eastern two-thirds of Texas, Gulf States.** In some botanical literature, this ground cover is described as a "noxious lawn weed" because it outcompetes grass in the

Horseherb *Calyptocarpus vailis*

shade. Funny, I thought that's exactly what we want a shady ground cover to do. It forms dense mats—eight to ten inches (20 to 25 cm) high—in shade with little or no water. You can mow it if you want a shorter mat, and it can take moderate amounts of foot traffic. It is evergreen where winter temperatures are above freezing.

5. *Carex* species. Dry wood and sedges. **Dry woods throughout North America.** Although the great majority of sedge species live in wetlands, there are a number of dry woodland sedges. Most have very narrow leaves and grow only about six inches (15 cm) high. Most are evergreen, at least in the South. Most are bunch sedges and must be allowed to seed out to form a lawn look. One that spreads by the roots and is being commercially grown is called Texas sedge *Carex texensis*. These woodland sedges are a worthy but heretofore unrecognized group horticulturally. There are many ideal for landscape use, such as cedar sedge *Carex planystachys*, eastern woodland sedge *Carex blanda*, Ruth's sedge *Carex ruthii*, purple sedge *Carex purpurifera*, low woodland sedge *Carex socialis*, and, in cool moist climates like Wisconsin, fox sedge *Carex vulpinoidea*. They can be told from grasses by their triangular stems.

6. *Chrysogonum virginianum*, green-and-gold. **Dry woodlands, pinelands, eastern U.S.** Very pretty, this one does best when neglected. In too much shade, it strains toward the sun. Too much water, and it gets sick. Partial shade on well-drained soil is just right. The southern variety produces a two-to-six-inch-high (5-to-15-cm) mass, while the northern green-and-gold is clump-forming and grows to sixteen inches (40 cm). It doesn't matter that it is not evergreen, because you want it to spend the winter covered with a mulch of autumn leaves.

7. *Ericameria laricifolia*, turpentinebush. **Piñon/juniper woodlands to creosote scrub between two thousand and six thousand feet (610 and 1,830 m) in Chihuahuan, Sonoran, and eastern Mojave Deserts.** A beautiful natural ground cover in desert foothills around El Paso, Tucson, Phoenix, and Las Vegas, turpentinebush has golden yellow flowers after rains. The small dark leaves smell like turpentine if you rub them between your fingers. About knee-high, it can be grown in masses or scattered thickly among taller, more widely spaced desert shrubs and trees. The less water you give it, the shorter it will stay. It likes full sun or morning shade and well-drained sand, granite, clay, loam, or limestone.

8. *Geum canadense*, white avens. **Nova Scotia to South Dakota to Georgia to Texas.** This is a great one to start off with if you have hard, undernourished soil. White avens is a pioneer plant—that is, it goes in first and holds the soil until such time as conditions improve for other plants. It displays white blooms in late spring, and can grow to eighteen inches (50 cm) high when in flower. It's mowable, and does well in full to partial shade. Individual plants aren't very long-lived, but a healthy colony can last for decades. The barbed

seeds stick to clothing, but this is not a problem if the flowers and seeds are mowed off in spring and again in early summer, which keeps the whole colony ankle high.

9. *Iris douglasiana*, Douglas iris. Coastal prairie and mixed evergreen forests, Santa Barbara, California, north to Oregon, below three thousand feet (915 m). Very handsome and very easy to grow, it likes full or partial shade, or even full sun. It thrives in southern California on just one or two deep waterings per month during the dry season. In the shade, or farther north, it needs even less. Hybridizing with other irises in its northern range produce three-inch (8-cm) flowers in white, cream, purple, lavender, blue, or rose.

Douglas iris *Iris douglasiana*

10. *Mitchella repens*, partridgeberry. Rich hardwood forests, pine-oak-hickory woodlands, stream banks, hammocks, eastern North America. White, fragrant blooms appear (in pairs) in late spring to fall, followed by red half-inch (13-mm) fruits (also in pairs) in late fall and winter. Good in full shade or full sun, it's extremely adaptable and easy to grow. Height is less than four inches (10 cm).

11. *Oenothera speciosa*, Mexican evening primrose. Southern Great Plains, infrequent in Chihuahuan Desert. It can be used as a low-growing ground cover in deep shade with summer irrigation to prevent it from going dormant. It produces fewer flowers there, however. In semi-shade, it covers itself with pale to deep pink blooms for two months every spring. It grows six to twelve inches (15 to 30 cm) high, sometimes reaching twenty inches (50 cm).

**Mexican evening primrose
*Oenothera speciosa***

12. *Salvia lyrata*, lyreleaf sage. Meadows, thin woodlands, stable dunes in the eastern half of the U.S. Lyreleaf sage is a cinch to grow, making it a great choice for beginners. It's especially useful on clay or dry soils overlying limestone. It forms two-to-four-inch (5-to-10-cm) mats, with one-to-two-foot (30-to-60-cm) flowers. The leaves are evergreen, four to eight inches (10 to 20 cm) long, and dark green in the sun.

13. *Senecio aureus*, golden groundsel, a.k.a. butterweed, golden ragwort. Bogs, meadows, wetlands, pastures, eastern U.S. This one is becoming very popular. It likes full shade or full sun, forms a two-to-four-inch (5-to-10-cm) mat, and reaches two to three feet (60 to 90 cm) when in bloom. The flowers are yellow

with drooping one-inch (2.5-cm) petals, and profuse from early spring to summer. More drought tolerant and fully evergreen, golden groundsel (a.k.a. squawweed; *Senecio obovatus*) blooms about Easter time. It is native from Texas to Florida and Quebec. It is just beginning to catch on in Dallas, and it looks like it will be a favorite. A new Latin name for these senecios is *Packera*.

14. ***Symphoricarpos alba* var. *laevigatus*, canyon snowberry. Woods, stream banks, north-facing slopes below thirty-six hundred feet (1,100 m) from southwestern California to Alaska.** Excellent for holding a steep shady bank or as a carefree waist-high ground cover under a shade tree. Once established, it can naturalize. Maximum height is six feet (180 cm) tall, although the usual height is two feet by two feet (60 cm) wide. It produces clusters of white berries in the fall and winter that attract birds. Other snowberries are native all over North America in zones 4 to 7, and all are well worth using.

15. ***Tiarella cordifolia*, foamflower. Rich woods, eastern North America.** This dainty woodland ground cover has overlapping leaves and airy white spring flowers. In the South it is found only in the mountains, and heat-tolerant Wherry's foamflower *Tiarella cordifolia* var. *collina* is preferred. Wherry's foamflower has no stolons, so you need to plant a great many plants nine inches (23 cm) apart to make a solid cover. And then it stays put and never oversteps its bounds. Both foamflowers grow six inches (15 cm) tall, twelve to twenty inches (30 to 50 cm) when in flower. The midspring blooms are white one-to-six-inch (2.5-to-15-cm) spikes, and the leaves are evergreen.

The Rest of the Plant Palette

Shade Trees   The one category of native plants that most people are familiar with—even if they don't necessarily think of them as natives—is shade trees, that is, trees that reach at least fifty feet (15 m) in height at maturity, and often exceed 100 feet (30 m), depending on which part of the country you're in. Chances are good that if you bought an older home, there were at least two or three shade trees—maples, elms, or ashes—already well established on the lot. You may have grown up swinging on a tire tied to the sturdy branch of a venerable native oak. Nurseries that may not carry any other native plants will almost surely carry native trees.

Yet we've done a poor job of caring for these wonderful, often majestic, natives. The hickories have long been slighted by the nursery trade, and as a result aren't as well known and appreciated as they deserve. The American elm *Ulmus americana* and the American chestnut *Castanea dentata*, once prominent throughout the East, are today almost extinct, thanks to our penchant for importing exotic species we think will be better. In fact, the Dutch elm gave us Dutch elm disease, which wiped out a vast percentage of our American elms, and the Eurasian chestnut conveyed a blight that pretty much did in our American chestnut population.

The big problem with shade (or canopy) trees is that humans are an impatient species. When we buy a home with a bare lot, we want trees right away. Big trees. And we know that shade trees take a long time to grow. So we often settle for fast-growing "trash" trees that put on a good show for awhile, but then die after only ten to thirty years. Because we're a mobile society and most people don't live in a house that long, they don't worry about it. The beautiful irony is, when they move to a new house in a new state, they probably inherit the trash tree the previous owners planted.

The inescapable fact is, a shade tree takes time to develop. Lots of time. And the best answer I can give to someone who wonders if it's worthwhile is to relate a story I heard about a middle-aged woman who wanted to go to college and get a degree. She told her husband it would take four years. "Four years!" he exclaimed. "Do you know how old you'll be in four years?" His wife answered, "How old will I be in four years if I *don't* get my degree?"

A shade tree has to begin sometime, so what are you waiting for? Here are some tips on how to do it right:

1. Your impulse will be to buy the biggest one you can afford. You'll be that much closer to that wonderful shade, right? Wrong. Studies show that after five

Sugar maple *Acer saccharum*

Shumard oak *Quercus shumardii*

American beech *Fagus grandifolia*

years, all else being equal, a smaller nursery tree (five feet [1.5 m] tall) will be as big or bigger than the sixteen-footer (5 m) you planted. The trauma a tree suffers in being transplanted is especially hard on larger trees. They'll spend most of their energy during those first five years just rebuilding their root system. For this reason, the larger transplants have a high mortality rate.

2. Trees planted less than fifty feet (15 m) apart will grow tall and slender; those planted with more space between them will be broader and fuller.

3. Your transplant will need watering to get it established. The smaller trees will need this for only two years, while the larger trees will need lots of TLC for at least five years—assuming they last that long.

4. Make sure your transplant is guaranteed by the nursery. They'll probably insist on planting it themselves, and that's a good idea.

5. Whether you put it in or they do, pick the right time of the year to do the job. In the south, plant in cool weather, usually after the first fall rain. Summer transplants lose a lot of water from evaporation through the leaves, and have a tougher time making it. In the north, plant as soon as the soil has thawed in spring, so your tree will have the maximum time to grow roots before it has to face a ferocious winter. If you live where there is a rainy season, planting just before that season usually works best.

6. Shade trees grow at different rates. After ten years, for example, a hackberry will be twice as large as a live oak. But the hackberry will be dead in fifty years, while the oak can be around for centuries.

7. Remember, too, that faster growers have weaker or softer wood. And that's important to know if you live where the winds can really kick up.

8. If you're buying for fall color, it's best to shop in the fall, so you can see what you'll be getting. Of course, this isn't always a sure thing; trees can change their habits as they mature, and trees in pots can feel the cold differently from trees in the ground.

9. When planting the tree, be sure not to leave air pockets when you replace the soil. And be sure to plant the tree at the same depth it was used to. Too shallow and the roots will dry out, too deep and the top roots won't be able to breathe properly. Never pile dirt up over the flare of the trunk.

10. For best results, select the same trees you find growing naturally in woodlands near your home.

Ornamental Trees They don't provide very much shade, they aren't used for erosion control, and as a rule they aren't dense enough to screen the neighbor's ugly chain-link fence or deaden the din from the nearby highway. And they aren't sturdy enough to support a tree house. So, you may ask, what good are they?

As the name implies, ornamental trees are beautiful and should be welcomed into your landscape for that reason alone. The bonus is that bees, birds, and butterflies are attracted to their fruits and blossoms. Every yard should have at least one.

Ornamental trees are usually classified as understory trees; that's where you find many of them in the wild—growing under the taller canopy trees. In this woodsy setting, they tend to grow with the branches well spaced, but in a sunny landscape they fill out and become dense and well rounded, with a more profuse crop of fruits and flowers.

These trees come in single-trunk or multi-trunked varieties, and both need judicious pruning from time to time to keep them looking their best. Multitrunked ornamentals can be pruned to be single-trunked trees, which will grow taller.

Ornamental trees are useful in numerous gardening situations because of their small stature. They fit well into typical urban yards. You can put two or three different ones around a patio for variety and visual interest, and they work well around a pool because they won't block all the sunshine, and they won't drop a ton of leaves into the water. In large-scale landscapes, where they can be planted in drifts, or as understory in a woodland setting, they provide welcome splashes of seasonal color.

Native ornamental trees already in wide use are redbud *Cercis canadensis*, flowering dogwood *Cornus florida*, southern magnolia *Magnolia grandiflora*, serviceberry *Amelanchier × grandiflora*, yaupon holly *Ilex vomitoria*, and black locust *Robinia pseudoaccia*. The following profiles are a sampling of some lesser-known native ornamental trees that are beginning to find favor around the country.

1. *Acer spicatum*, **mountain maple. Mixed woods and copses from Saskatchewan to Ohio, Connecticut, and the mountains of Tennessee and North Carolina.** While the leaves turn a brilliant mottled orange in the fall, they are also very attractive in the warmer months. The flowers are clustered and develop as erect, fluffy pale green spikes. Very cold tolerant, this ornamental is also very resistant to the voracious gypsy moth. The tallest mountain maple found so far is sixty feet (18 m) and located in Michigan.

2. *Asimina triloba*, **pawpaw. Moist, well-drained woodlands in eastern U.S.** Born and bred southerners grew up singing "Pickin' up pawpaws and puttin' 'em in a basket." Its foot-long (30-cm) leaves can give a garden a tropical look. Pawpaw (a.k.a. Indian banana) handles full shade to full sun, but if you're planting one for the fruits, make sure it gets at least a half day of sun. Also, choose a cultivar; the sweetness and flavor will be more consistent.

3. *Cercidium floridum*, **blue paloverde. Washes below thirty-five hundred feet (1,070 m) in Sonoran and Colorado Deserts.** Paloverdes are the best-loved trees of the Sonoran Desert. Even without their lime green leaves or golden flowers, their light green trunks and branches are a distinctively handsome sight. Usual height is fifteen feet (4.5 m), but they can get to twenty-five feet (8 m) with the right conditions. The flowers are a source of nectar for bees and butterflies, and the seeds are eaten by doves.

4. *Chilopsis linearis*, **desert willow. Southern Colorado, Arizona and New Mexico, and west Texas.** Desert willow blooms from midspring to fall, making it a big favorite from Texas to the California coast. An old tree has graceful, thick, twisty trunks. The leaves give a lacy shade. It grows so quickly that you might have to prune it a few times the first year, but probably not at all by the fifth. Usual height is fifteen feet (4.5 m). Flower colors range from white to pink to rich purple. Good drainage is recommended. Hardiness is to zone 7.

5. *Chionanthus virginicus*, **fringe tree. Moist woodland edges from Ohio and Pennsylvania to the Gulf Coast.** This tree is spectacular in full bloom. The flowers are pure white and fragrant. Fall color is yellow. Usual height is twenty to thirty feet (6 to 9 m). Fringe tree seems to be cold hardy from zone 9 in Houston up into zone 4 in southern Quebec and Ontario. It must have acid soil, and it prefers lots of compost. The male trees are showier in flower, but the females produce dark blue fruits that attract wildlife, so one of each is a good idea.

6. *Cladrastic kentukea*, **yellowwood. Ozark and Appalachian cove forests and limestone ridges.** A handsome tree, easily fifty feet (15 m) tall or more, yellowwood prefers full sun, but can thrive on the edge of shade. The flowers look like white wisteria. Fall color is yellow to golden orange. The name reflects that the root bark was used to make a yellow dye. Although limited to a small range, probably because it cannot thrive in tall eastern forests and is not adapted to a fire regimen, yellowwood grows well in sunny gardens from zones 3 to 7 in the eastern half of the continent.

7. *Cotinus obovatus*, **American smoke tree. Limestone soils from Kentucky to Alabama to the Hill Country of Texas.** Much prettier than the European smoke tree, American smoke tree has so many teeny flowers in the spring that it looks like it's wreathed in a cloud of pink. Fall color is deep orange to gold. Good drainage is essential. Height ranges from fifteen to thirty feet (4.5 to 9 m), depending on richness of soil. This tree is supposed to grow slowly and live over a century.

8. *Crataegus viridis*, **green hawthorn. Floodplain woodlands from Delaware and Indiana to Florida and central Texas.** Sometimes thornless, this hawthorn is covered with white flowers in the spring and bright red fruits in the fall. The fluted, twisting trunk is the color of apple-cinnamon ice cream. Height is from fifteen to thirty-five feet

Fringe tree *Chionanthus virginicus*

(4.5 to 9 m) tall with a spread of twenty-five to fifty feet (8 to 15 m). The leaves host butterfly larvae, and the fruits are such a favorite with songbirds that they are gobbled up within a few days of ripening.

9. *Euonymus atropurpureus*, **wahoo. Mesic woodlands from Toronto south to northern Tennessee and west to Kansas.** One of the most shade-tolerant woody plants, wahoo can also grow well in full sun. Its most attractive feature is its pink popcorn-shaped fruit capsules, which can add a rustic touch in floral arrangements. Plant it with witch hazel, and you'll get an exciting early winter combination of yellow flowers and red fruits. Fall color is bright to dark red.

Possumhaw *Ilex decidua*

10. *Ilex decidua*, **possumhaw. Virginia to Illinois to Gulf of Mexico.** This ornamental does well in dappled or part shade, but needs at least six hours of sun per day to become fully covered with bright red fall and winter fruits. Since the trees are either male or female, you'll want to plant a male (or know that some are nearby) to assure that the female flowers become pollinated to make berries.

11. *Leucaena retusa*, **goldenball leadtree. Southeast Arizona, lower New Mexico, into central Texas.** A fairly quick grower in a garden setting, goldenball leadtree gets its name from its bright golden fluffy flowers, which can be very fragrant after a rain. Watering once or twice a month will give you almost continuous blooms throughout the warm season. Usual height is fifteen feet (4.5 m).

12. *Magnolia virginiana*, **sweet bay. Coastal plain and outer Piedmont from Delaware to Texas.** Sweet bay is unique among the southern magnolias in that it will not only tolerate soggy soil, it actually likes it. The lemony-fragrant velvet white flowers appear in spring. The silvery white undersides to the leaves make this tree sparkle in a breeze. In zone 9, sweet bay is evergreen most winters. The usual height is sixty feet (18 m), and it can occasionally reach one hundred feet (30 m). The fruits are dark red cones with bright red seeds.

13. *Olneya tesota*, **ironwood. Desert washes and creosote scrub in lower Sonoran and Colorado Deserts.** Ironwood is not fond of cold weather and freezes back at 20 degrees Fahrenheit (−7 degrees Celsius). That's why it is used as an indicator plant of climates warm enough to grow orange trees. It has a silvery trunk and leaves, and some trees have rosy flowers. Very drought

Ironwood *Olneya tesota*

Sourwood *Oxydendrum arboreum*

tolerant, ironwood likes well-drained dry, decomposed granite, sand, or clay loam. Its usual height is fifteen feet (4.5 m) tall.

14. *Oxydendrum arboreum*, **sourwood. Southeastern U.S. below fifty-five hundred feet (1,675 m).** Of all the trees Sally and I saw in our southeast travels, this one impressed us the most. It's outstanding when in flower, even when seen at highway speeds. In the fall, the red foliage almost always elicits a "Wow!" If you can't find one in a nursery, it's easily grown from seed. It grows twenty to thirty feet (6 to 9 m) tall, and is happiest in full sun or partial shade.

15. *Viburnum nudum*, **possumhaw viburnum. Edges of wet woodlands from east Texas to Connecticut.** Without pruning, this small tree is a large shrub ten to twenty feet (3 to 6 m) tall. The flower clusters are creamy white. The clusters of fruits make this viburnum a favorite.

Over several weeks in the summer they change from cream to pink to lavender to deep blue. There are many other handsome native viburnums, some very drought tolerant. Fall colors are often pink, mauve, and purple instead of red and gold. Butterflies visit the flowers and birds eat the fruits.

Short Perennials We have many native perennial flowers that grow less than knee-high, many only ankle-high. These are useful for edging flower beds or for making permanent low beds of color where we presently plant pansies and impatiens, where we used to plant marigolds and petunias, before the bugs beat us at that game. A flower bed that is made up of a variety of short perennials that come into bloom at different times is healthier. Weeding is a bore, but it is no more expensive than tilling and buying new plants two or three times a year. Plus, think what you could save on watering and landfill! For a successful planting, make sure that you group these perennials according to their moisture preferences: wet, moist, well-drained, or dry. Many of these short perennials are native to the southwestern deserts, and they bloom whenever there is rain or very light irrigation. The more northern ones usually spread by underground roots and bloom early in the spring.

1. *Baileya multiradiata,* **desert marigold. Dry loose soil in Chihuahuan, Sonoran, and Mojave Deserts.** Short, neat, ever blooming, and easily the most dependable and useful of the desert flowers. It can be the mainstay of a flower bed or the unifying color in a patch of existing or revegetated desert. Individual plants can live an average of two years.

2. *Berlandiera lyrata,* **chocolate daisy. Kansas to Colorado, Arizona to Mexico.** Yes, it does smell like chocolate. It has a fuzzy maroon (sometimes orange) center that is surrounded by a green setting of leaflike material after the petals fall. Likes part shade to full sun, and well-drained sand, clay, loam, or caliche. Butterflies like it a lot.

3. *Callirhoe involucrata,* **winecup. Dry soil from Minnesota to Utah south to Mexico.** Think of winecup as an especially long-blooming bulb. It looks magnificent cascading over a wall or down a rocky slope. It has green rosettes in winter, and in warm climates it sends out prostrate stems in the spring that bloom throughout April and May. It then shrinks back to small rosettes. With supplemental watering, it can bloom all summer.

Winecup *Callirhoe involucrata*

Chocolate daisy *Berlandiera lyrata*

4. *Calylophus hartwegii,* **sundrops. Dry soils from Wyoming to Mexico.** Large, translucent yellow flowers in the evening primrose family seem to glow with light, almost hiding the narrow grayish green foliage. Blooms start in spring, and will

continue all summer with occasional irrigation. Usually less than a foot (30 cm) high, sundrops can get two feet (61 cm) wide in rich soil. Good drainage is a must. There are numerous species of *Calylophus*, and all of them are garden-worthy.

5. *Campanula rotundifolia*, **harebell. Moist to dry semi-shade from Canada down to New Jersey, Indiana, and Iowa.** Pale blue to lavender bells make this a favorite in the spring. The plants usually form small mounds less than a foot (30 cm) tall.

Harebell *Campanula rotundifolia*

6. *Coreopsis auriculata*, **eared coreopsis, or dwarf tickseed. Rich woods, eastern red cedar habitats in southeast U.S.** The ones we have seen in shade gardens seemed to be straining toward the sun so hard that the stems were almost horizontal. Short and dainty, this coreopsis prefers full sun and rich, acid soil. The ground-hugging leaves stay green all winter.

7. *Erigeron modestus*, **plains fleabane. Dry soil from Arizona to Texas and north to Kansas.** This six-to-nine-inch (15-to-25-cm) mound of white daisies blooms for months. A somewhat short-lived perennial, ours usually lasted only two to three years. The white petals are very narrow, and the flat yellow center is quite large in comparison. There are several species of showy, short fleabanes, and nearly every part of North America has at least one.

8. *Geranium maculatum*, **wild geranium. Moist soil from Maine to Manitoba and south to northeast Oklahoma and Georgia.** Wild geranium spreads underground to make masses of purple flowers each spring. It lasts for years as long as it doesn't get too much water. It does best in light shade.

9. *Heuchera sanguinea*, **Arizona coralbells. Moist soil in mountains of Arizona and northern Mexico.** Flowers are deep pink with a hint of orange. This species is often hybridized with California's white-flowered island alumroot *Heuchera maxima*. It prefers light shade.

10. *Iris cristata*, **dwarf iris or crested iris. Rich woodlands in the southeastern U.S.** The flowers are surprisingly large in relation to the overall plant, and they all bloom at once. It's easy to grow and very popular with southern gardeners. The flowers are blue to dark blue, and sometimes white, although rarely so in the wild. Dwarf iris likes rich, moist, acid soil and full to partial shade.

11. *Lilium philadelphicum*, western red lily. Moist soils from the Canadian prairies south to Arizona, the trans-Pecos in Texas, and Arkansas. This three-to-four-inch (8-to-10-cm) red orange lily is as showy as any hybridized nursery lily, but it is only knee-high. It loves full sun and rich moist soil. As a native, it is a prairie flower growing with big bluestem and able to withstand fire and live for decades. It blooms in early spring.

12. *Lithospermum canescens*, hoary puccoon. Well-drained soil in prairies from Pennsylvania to Saskatchewan south to Georgia, Missouri, and northeast Oklahoma. The flowers are deep orange yellow and the leaves are silvery green. Average height is six to eighteen inches (15 to 45 cm). Bloom time is late spring or early summer. Plant about nine inches (25 cm) apart for a solid cover, but it is better to alternate it with a flower or ornamental grass that blooms late summer to fall. That way you get bedding-plant color for several months each year with no replanting.

13. *Melampodium leucanthemum*, blackfoot daisy. Limestone and calcareous soils in Kansas, Colorado, Arizona, Texas, and Mexico. In a garden, with compost and occasional watering, it will get one foot (30 cm) tall and eighteen inches (45 cm) wide. If you like to mass some plants, this one is a good choice. It thrives in part shade, full sun, and as an added bonus, in sunshine it releases a strong wild-honey scent.

14. *Oenothera caespitosa*, fragrant evening primrose. Stony slopes between four thousand and seventy-five hundred feet (1,220 and 2,290 m) in Chihuahuan, Sonoran, and Mojave Deserts, and the Great Basin. It has sweetly scented spring blooms that open at sunset and stay open until the temperature gets hot. The three-to-four-inch (8-to-10-cm) flowers are white when they first appear, but turn pink just before they fold up and fall off. It does well on one or two waterings a month, and likes full sun to partial shade. This primrose attracts butterflies, hummingbirds, and white-lined hawk moths. The leafy rosettes are often evergreen and multiply to form dense colonies.

15. *Stokesia laevis*, Stokes aster. Wet to moist soils, sand preferred, coastal plain east of the Mississippi River. Growing this one is easy. Despite its native range, it seems to be winter hardy to zone 5. It blooms best in full sun and looks great in a flower garden teamed up with purple coneflower, butterflyweed, and other popular perennials. Stokes aster grows to a height of twelve to eighteen inches (30 to 45 cm) and sports blue, lavender, and white blooms from late spring to early summer, occasionally lasting until fall.

Blackfoot daisy *Melampodium leucanthemum*

Tall Perennials Perennial flowers from knee height to over one's head are very dramatic and make a sophisticated flower garden. Several native perennials, short-lived perennials, and biennials are already well known in the nursery trade and have been found in the major catalogs for over a generation, such as Black-eyed Susan *Rudbeckia hirta*, Oswego tea *Monardka didyma*, purple coneflower *Echinacea purpurea*, fall obedient plant *Physostegia virginiana*, summer phlox *Phlox paniculata*, and New England aster *Aster novae-angliae*. Some recently hybridized native perennials are *Rudbeckia* 'Goldsturm' and *Rudbeckia* 'Herbstsonne,' returned to us from German horticulturists. But with the rise of nurseries that specialize in native plants, many selections of our finest tall native flowers are becoming available for the first time. This sampling will give you an idea of the treats in store once you start exploring our tall perennial flowers. Most of these are native to tallgrass prairies, so they prefer full sun to less than a half day of shade.

1. *Aquilegia chrysantha*, **yellow columbine. Moist soil in mountains from Colorado to Mexico.** This grows best in sand and rocky soils on slopes, but can do very well in improved garden soil on clay as long as the drainage is good. If you plant it in plenty of shade and give it a tiny bit of extra watering, it will be fully evergreen.

2. *Aster azureus* (*Aster oolentangiensis*), **skyblue aster. Moist but well-drained soil from the Great Lakes to the Gulf of Mexico.** The small, scattered daisylike flowers are an indescribable shade of pale blue that seems to leap to your attention. The whole plant is airy and about two feet (60 cm) tall and eighteen inches (45 cm) wide. Bloom time is late summer to midfall. A great companion plant is showy goldenrod *Solidago speciosa*. These two can make a fall garden the highlight of the year. Both do particularly well in sandy soil.

3. *Baptisia alba*, **white baptisia or white wild indigo. Northern tallgrass prairies and savannas, sandhills, flatwoods, post oak woods, and pinelands in the eastern two-thirds of North America.** The most striking thing about white baptisia is the dark blue gray stems that set off its white flowers. This gives the plant an unusual, some even call it a sophisticated, appearance. In a perennial bed, plant low-growing downy phlox or pink coreopsis at its feet. It likes full to a half day of sun.

4. *Echinacea pallida*, **pale coneflower. Well-drained tallgrass prairies and savannas.** Its narrow, drooping petals

Yellow columbine *Aquilegia chrysantha*

range from pale pink to rose, are three to five inches (8 to 13 cm) across, with green, red, purple, or brown globular centers. In its native range, it blooms from late spring to early summer. It likes acid soil that can be either moist or dry, and full sun. Bees are very fond of this coneflower.

5. ***Eryngium yuccifolium*, eryngo or rattlesnake master. Moist to dry prairie soils in eastern half of U.S.** Eryngo is grown for its leaves, not its pale flowers. Use it where you want a strong vertical accent in your garden. But it needs to be a solitary focal point; several of them scattered up and down a border would be too overpowering. This summer-blooming perennial is tolerant of a wide range of habitats. It can be in dry soil, where it will remain relatively short, or it can be in an almost wet habitat, where it will grow to a height of three to four feet (90 to 120 cm), occasionally six feet (180 cm).

6. ***Filipendula rubra*, queen of the prairie. Wet soils and pond edges in a range centered around the Great Lakes.** Queen of the prairie is rare or extinct in much of its native range, but it is such a spectacular flower that it has long been used in local gardens. About five feet (1.5 m) tall and proudly upright, it has a pink plume of flowers the size of a stick of cotton candy you would get at the state fair. It can be grown in rich garden soil if watered regularly. (Did you know that many of our ordinary garden flowers were originally bog plants?) Queen of the prairie does not require strongly acid soil, but it does need at least a half day of sun. Bloom time is early to midsummer.

7. ***Gaura lindheimeri*, butterfly gaura. Gumbo prairies in southeast and south-central Texas, and pinelands in southern Louisiana.** A "see-through" perennial, it has slender stems that are almost leafless. The fragrant flowers seem to float off these stems like little white butterflies. The roots like both moist sandy loam and moist black clay. It does best in full sun, although a little shade is fine. While its normal height is two to three feet (60 to 90 cm), it can reach as tall as eight feet (260 cm).

8. ***Helianthus angustifolius*, swamp sunflower. Wet to moist soils in eastern U.S.** In some places, it's common to see swamp sunflower growing in magnificent golden swaths covering a half acre or more. Accent it with the coppery

Swamp sunflower *Helianthus angustifolius*

plums of sugarcane plumegrass and the blue of wild ageratum. It is easy to grow and control in a semidry environment. Usual height is one and a half to five feet (50 to 150 cm), and on rare occasions it can reach ten feet (3 m). It likes moist to wet acid soil, and full sun.

9. *Liatris pycnostachya*, **cattail gayfeather or prairie blazing star. Wet to moist soils around Mississippi River basin and tall-grass prairies.** There are numerous gayfeathers worth your attention. Cattail gayfeather likes very acid sand, and tolerates poor drainage. But give it rich organic matter and too much water, and its upright posture becomes floppy. It grows two to five feet (60 to 150 cm) tall, and does best in full sun.

10. *Monarda fistulosa*, **beebalm or wild bergamot. Meadows and post oak woodlands east of the Rocky Mountains.** This is a superb garden flower, well adapted over a large portion of the country. It is long-lived and easy-going, thriving under almost any conditions, including extreme heat. The flowers are pink or lavender, and can bloom from late spring to midsummer. It also makes a tasty herbal tea and is

Cattail gayfeather *Liatris pycnostachya*

Wild bergamot *Monarda fistulosa*

reputed to draw the poison out of a bee sting—hence its name.

11. *Penstemon digitalis*, **Mississippi penstemon or smooth white beard-tongue. Meadows, thin woodlands in eastern half of North America; probably only native to Mississippi River basin and naturalized everywhere else.** If you live in the coastal plains or along the Mississippi River where clay loam and poor drainage make it difficult to grow flowers, this one will work. We saw masses of it there blooming profusely—and not in raised beds, either. It thrives in full to partial sun and grows to a height of eighteen inches (46 cm). White blooms with purple accents (guidelines for bees) appear in late spring and stay around for about four weeks.

12. *Rudbeckia laciniata*, **wild goldenglow. Wet to moist soils from eastern U.S. to Arizona.** One of the coneflowers, this dramatic plant is often well over six feet (180 cm) tall and three to five feet (90 to 150 cm) wide. The tall, dark fingerlike cones in the center are encircled by a spiral of large yellow petals that bloom in sequence for several weeks. The leaves are large and coarse, shading the ground at the base of the plant. Full sun is best, but a few hours of shade is tolerated. A commercial hybrid of this plant developed in Germany is called 'Herbstsonne.'

13. *Solidago nemoralis*, **gray goldenrod. Dry, well-drained soils in North America east of the Rocky Mountains, from Canada to the Edward's Plateau in central Texas.** The wild goldenrod most people see is a weedy specimen whose roots can devour a whole garden. However, we have many beautiful native goldenrods that we ought to be developing horticulturally. They do not cause hay fever, but bloom in the fall at the same time as ragweed. The flowers are bright to pale yellow, rich in nectar, and usually covered with butterflies. Gray goldenrod is long-lived, drought tolerant, fairly short in stature at two to three feet (60 to 90 cm), and has well-mannered roots. The leaves are fuzzy, which gives them a gray green color. Showy goldenrod *Solidago speciosa* is native to moist sandy soils in the heart of the United States. There are several goldenrods that prefer shade. Zigzag goldenrod *Solidago flexicaulis* grows under bur oaks on clay soil or limestone from Canada to Arkansas and Virginia, centering on the Great Lakes region. It is especially handsome with heartleaf aster *Aster cordifolius*.

14. *Thermopsis villosa*, **Carolina bushpea. Moist clearings in the southern Appalachians.** Carolina bushpea grows naturally in forest clearings in the mountains, but if you don't happen to live there, no problem. It accommodates itself to gardens all over the South, even in the coastal plain. It likes full sun and moist, rich, acid soil. The blooms are yellow to pale cream on four-to-twelve-inch (10-to-30-cm) spikes, and appear in late spring. Its height—three to five feet (90 to 150 cm)—makes it a dominant member of a garden. Give it plenty of room; it doesn't like to be crowded.

15. *Zizia aurea*, **golden Alexanders. Moist to dryish soil in eastern North America.** This yellow spring flower is about two feet (61 cm) tall and does best in zones 4 to 6. A more drought-tolerant but less heat-tolerant version is heartleaf Alexanders *Zizia aptera*, which grows across Canada and down the Appalachians and the Rockies. The pale green seed and dark green leaves make this plant handsome even when it's not in bloom.

Ornamental Grasses   When many people think of grass, they think of lawns. Surprise! There are many native bunchgrasses that serve as accents and add a wonderful texture to a landscape. Here are just a few.

1. *Andropogon glomeratus*, **bushy bluestem. Southeastern U.S. to California and the West Indies.** This grass will tolerate the overwatering typi-

cal of most home landscapes. In winter, it turns to a coppery orange; in the fall it is equally showy, with large fluffy spires of silky white flowers. Its usual height is two to five feet (60 to 150 cm). It likes sand, loam, and clay, either acid or calcareous, and can handle poor drainage.

2. *Bouteloua curtipendula*, **sideoats grama. Canada to Argentina.** Sideoats grama is a comfortable size and shape

Landscaping Revolutionary: Ron Gass

Noah Webster was wrong.

The famed lexicographer defined *desert* as "a desolate or forbidding area." Clearly, he never had the opportunity to chat with Ron Gass, owner of Mountain States Wholesale Nursery in Glendale, Arizona. Ron

would have quickly set him straight.

For Ron Gass, the desert is a wondrous place, full of color and vitality and immense possibilities. He is a quiet-spoken, easygoing man, yet when he talks about the desert he can become

almost passionate. One of the reasons for this passion is the native desert plants that he has grown, collected, and championed for over thirty years. Perhaps no one else has done so much to alter the mind-set of homeowners, nursery owners, and municipalities alike with regard to desert landscaping.

Gass preaches the gospel of drought-tolerant, low-maintenance natives everywhere he travels—and that amounts to over forty thousand miles annually as he roams the deserts of the Southwest and even down into Mexico. But he doesn't set up a tent for his brand of proselytizing; he makes converts one at a time, talking one day to a nursery owner in Las Cruces, the next to a

for use as a garden accent. The seed provides excellent bird food from summer into the winter. It stays low during the spring, making it a good grass to use with spring wildflowers. Put it in well-drained sand, loam, clay, or limestone. It can reach six feet (180 cm) tall, but its more usual height is two to three feet (60 to 90 cm).

3. *Digitaria californica*, **Arizona cottontop. Rocky hills and grasslands between one thousand and six thousand feet (305 and 1,830 m) in Sonoran and Chihuanhuan Deserts to the Gulf of Mexico.** When in bloom, Arizona cottontop is as showy as any garden flower. The cottonlike spikes top a profusion of wiry stems and create a bouquet of

county extension agent in west Texas, then to a landscape architect in Tucson, and the next day to a customer at his own nursery.

Until recently, whenever Ron was off on his travels—which can occasionally run to as many as seven to ten days on the road—his wife and business partner, Maureen, held down the fort, taking on the day-to-day chores required in running a large and successful commercial nursery, from potting plants to dealing with customers. Today, Maureen is the proud holder of a degree in nursing, so her involvement at the nursery is now limited to overseeing the books. Friends describe the two as a perfect combination, Ron being the visionary, the man with the mission,

while Maureen balances her husband's idealism by being there to dot the i's and cross the t's.

There are many throughout the Southwest who credit Ron with inspiring and encouraging them. Landscape architect Steve Martino, of Tempe, Arizona, even goes so far as to call Ron "a saint, someone you want your kids to grow up to be like." Steve says Ron opened his eyes to native desert plants over twenty years ago. "He has the rare gift of answering a dumb question without letting on that it's dumb."

From time to time, Ron's "saintliness" has been put to the test. Gregg Starr, owner of Starr Nursery in Tucson, remembers a time when he and Ron went plant

hunting in a remote desert area. "We were collecting seed from a nolina . . . a yucca that grows like a tree down in Mexico," Starr says. "I was standing on Ron's shoulders to reach the seed stalk, and my hands were getting cut up pretty badly on the razor-sharp leaf edges. Ron kept up a line of encouraging chatter, keeping my flagging spirits up, and promising to take care of the cuts as soon as I got down.

"It was only as I was getting down from his shoulders that I noticed a swarm of angry bees buzzing close to his face. They'd been there the whole time, but he was more concerned about *my* safety than his own. That, in a nutshell," says Starr, "is Ron Gass."

white that is dazzling when backlit. Since it is nearly evergreen, it works just fine as a ground cover. Extra watering will make it lush, but perhaps taller than you'd like. Normal clump size is two feet by two feet (60 cm), but it's been known to grow to four feet by five feet (120 by 150 cm).

4. *Hierchloe*, **sweetgrass. Cold, moist prairies in northern North America.** This is a species that is native all around the northern part of our globe. The genetic material found in Europe is also native to Nova Scotia, but most of our native sweetgrass is slightly different. Sweetgrass Gardens, a Native American nursery in Hagersville, Ontario, sells our native sweetgrass as plants and seed, as this grass is important in Native American rituals. The fragrance of the leaves, either green or dried, can freshen a room or a drawer. This grass is also beautiful in the garden. Less than knee-high, it is finely textured, upright, and a bright lime green. It travels by root to make a mass planting.

5. *Hystrix patula,* **bottlebrush grass. Rich woodlands in northeastern North America.** Related to rye and wheat, bottlebrush grass grows about four feet (120 cm) tall and prefers the sunny edge of shade. The flower heads resemble a giant bottle brush, and they have a way of catching the light and glowing golden even when surrounding leaves are in shadow. Although bottlebrush grass likes rich, moist garden soil, it cannot handle poor drainage or being overwatered.

6. *Leymus condensatus*, **elymus or giant wild rye. Coastal sage scrub, chaparral, scrub oak woodlands below forty-five hundred feet (1,375 m), from west-central California to Mexico.** This is a bunchgrass that forms a tidy, well-mannered clump that is welcome in the most fastidious person's flower garden. It

grows in both full sun and full shade, and everything in between. Its wide bluish leaves are a bold accent among delicate-leaved red columbine or dark, glossy-leaved evergreen currant. Its maximum size is a clump twelve feet by eight feet (370 by 240 cm). A massed planting of this grass also makes a striking waist-high ground cover.

7. *Melica nitens*, **melicgrass. Dry soil from Wisconsin to Mexico.** This is a lovely cool-season grass. The leaves are green all winter, and the abundant clusters of spring flowers are white enough to show up well, even in the shade of an old live oak tree. This grass likes well-drained loam, both acid and calcareous. It is rarely seen in full sun, preferring dappled to partial shade. Melicgrass is normally in the two-to-three-foot (60-to-90-cm) range.

8. *Muhlenbergia capillaris*, **gulf muhly. Prairies and forest openings from Massachusetts to Mexico.** In the autumn, when it turns deep pink, this grass is stunning backlit by a rising or setting sun. In the spring, it is an ideal backdrop for wildflowers. Growing from one and a half to two and a half feet (45 to 75 cm) tall, gulf muhly likes full sun or partial shade, and

Gulf muhly *Muhlenbergia capillaris*

sand, loam, or clay; seasonally poor drainage is OK.

9. *Muhlenbergia dumosa*, **bamboo muhly. Lower elevations in the Sonoran Desert.** This grass is unusual. For one thing, it tolerates full shade. For another, its leaves and stems are a pale, golden khaki all year; it's never all green. The flowers and seed heads resemble asparagus foliage, and this delicate "misty" look lasts for months. Mass it under a tree or use it as an accent—a spineless alternative to sotol or yucca. It can form a five-foot-by-six-foot (150-by-180-cm) clump.

10. *Muhlenbergia lindheimeri*, **Lindheimer's muhly. Endemic to Texas.** This is a handsome grass for the calcareous soils in the center of the state, and is commonly used as an accent instead of non-native pampas grass. It's preferable, among other reasons, because the leaves are softer, so you won't get scratched when you cut it back. Usual height is two to five feet (60 to 150 cm). Plant it in well-drained limestone, sand, or clay, and make sure it gets full sun or partial shade.

11. *Muhlenbergia rigens*, **deergrass. Canyons, chaparral, and woodlands between twenty-five hundred and seven thousand feet (760 and 2,130 m) in southern California coastal ranges, and in the Mojave and Chihuahuan Deserts.** Even when it's dormant, deergrass remains upright, well shaped, and handsomely colored—khaki with faint undertones of green. It's rugged, and even in desert gardens needs only a little irrigation to look its best. Some people use it as a ground cover, but somehow the clumps have a way of standing out as individuals and never quite get together to form a mass. This is a full-sun grass that needs well-drained sand, clay, or decomposed granite with low organic content.

12. *Saccharum giganteum*, **sugarcane plumegrass. New York to Cuba.** The big feathery flowers bloom dark red or coral and then fade to pink or apricot, ending up silvery with seed. As with most ornamental grasses, backlighting delivers the full benefit of color. If you cut it when it's still in flower, it makes a terrific dried arrangement. This is a full-sun grass that does best in moist sand, loam, and clay. It can take poor drainage as well. Usual height is six feet (180 cm).

13. *Sorghastrum nutans*, **Indiangrass. Canada to Mexico.** Indiangrass loves moist rich soils and responds well to supplemental watering. It has large, broad, blueish green blades and bright golden fall flowers. This grass makes a spectacular accent in a tallgrass prairie garden, or teamed up with gulf muhly.

Indiangrass *Sorghastrum nutans*

Usual height is three to five feet (90 to 150 cm), but it can reach eight feet (240 cm) in some conditions. Grow it in dappled or partial shade, or full sun.

14. *Sporobolus heterolepsis*, **prairie dropseed. Well-drained moist to dry prairies from Manitoba to Oklahoma and adjacent states.** One of our most beautiful native grasses, prairie dropseed forms knee-high clumps of very narrow leaves that are a lovely golden green color. The flowers are airy and delicate, not colorful, but fragrant. They remind some people of hot buttered popcorn. As a specimen plant or as a mass planting, prairie dropseed is well mannered, long-lived, and always elegant.

Mexican feathergrass *Stipa tenuissima*

Prairie dropseed *Sporobolus heterolepsis*

15. *Stipa tenuissima*, **Mexican feathergrass. Texas trans-Pecos and New Mexico all the way down to Argentina.** This ornamental forms a graceful "vase" of needle-fine, yellowish green leaves. The taller flowers, equally slender, start out silver and fade to gold. The result is a clump that is greenish at the base and silver or golden at the tips, and looks great green or dormant. It likes full sun or partial shade, and well-drained loam, sand, or clay—either acid or calcareous. Relatively low-growing, it is normally one to two feet (30 to 60 cm) tall, and on rare occasions three feet (90 cm).

Chapter 5

EXOTICS: A DOUBLE-EDGED SWORD

"If dandelions were rare and fragile, people would knock themselves out to pay $14.95 a plant, raise them by hand in greenhouses, and form dandelion societies and all that. But they are everywhere and don't need us and kind of do what they please. So we call them 'weeds' and murder them at every opportunity."

Robert Fulghum
All I Really Need to Know I Learned in Kindergarten

There was a time when, if someone mentioned "exotic" plants, I pictured something out of *Little Shop of Horrors*: a garishly colored vegetational wonder from some faraway land like Madagascar or the jungles of Tasmania, a plant with flamboyant plumes and menacing ten-foot-long (3-m) tendrils that lured small birds and mammals into its gaping maw. Y'know . . . *exotic*!

When landscape designer Kitty Taylor created her own garden in Colliersville, Tennessee, it included both natives and good exotics. This section of the garden features antique roses, dianthus, and bulb iris.

But in the gardening world, *exotic* has a more prosaic meaning; the word simply refers to the fact that the plant comes from someplace else. In other words, it is not native to wherever we are talking about. And, while some of these exotics *are* on the flamboyant side, most are pretty ordinary looking. Queen Anne's lace, for example, is an exotic weed that came here from Eurasia and North Africa—but it doesn't inspire open-mouthed stares or double takes. In fact, it's so commonly seen growing in the wild, many people think it's a native.

A Bum Rap

No surprise, Sally and I are enthusiastic about natives, and we've written numerous books and articles about them. And it never seems to fail; someone will write an irate letter to the magazine or newspaper, or to our publisher, accusing us of being unfair—even hostile—to exotics!

So let's set the record straight on this point. We have *never* put down exotics in the general sense. Our former home landscape back in Dallas was at least 30 percent exotic. Of that number, some were native to other parts of Texas, some were native to other parts of the country, and a few were from other parts of the world. What they had in common with our natives was beauty, drought tolerance, and good manners, i.e., they were noninvasive.

There are many good exotics and, depending on what part of the country you're in, you can enjoy them to your heart's content. (Just don't plant them in a preserved natural habitat, such as a prairie, and destroy the indigenous integrity of that habitat.) But the thing to remember is, no exotic is going to work *everywhere*, despite what some plant catalogs imply. What you have to do is find out the native origin of the exotic you like, and determine how well suited or unsuited it will be to your conditions. Plants native to the tropical zones of South America will not be well suited to colder climates, just as plants that are native to northern regions of Eurasia will do poorly in the Southwest. It's common sense, really.

But how can you know the native range of your exotics? Reference books are too general. We are told that gardenias, for example, are native to China. But where in China? That's like saying a plant is native to the United States. The reference books also tell you which zone or zones a plant will find hospitable, but look at a zone map and you'll see that each zone covers numerous different elevations, soil types, and rainfall conditions. They can't all be ideal. Zone information tends to be helpful in the northeast, but it's just one small part of the equation elsewhere.

The truth is, most reference books assume you will have to alter the growing conditions to suit your exotics. That's what high-maintenance conventional gardening is all about. And picking exotics that will be xeriscapic in your area is difficult; the information, in most cases, is nonexistent. One of your best bets is to ask your local water department for a list of drought-tolerant plants for your area. And just because your nursery is selling certain exotics doesn't mean they are automatically well adapted to local conditions.

As a professional landscape designer, Sally always advises her clients to *use what works*. And if you have a few exotics you've always loved, relax—you don't have to give them up when you join the landscaping revolution. Unless . . .

Ipheion and schoolhouse lily are two exotic bulbs that do well in the southeast, surviving without watering or upkeep.

Peonies are often found in old neglected gardens where they have lived on their own for decades, yet they do not invade wilderness areas.

◆ They require an inordinate amount of work and natural resources to keep them alive. This accounts for a large percentage of standard nursery stock, especially annuals.

or

◆ They are invasive and harmful to the environment.

Let's look at both categories a little more closely.

The TMT Exotics   TMT stands for Too Much Trouble, and these exotics make up the core of the lemon landscape we talked about earlier. For starters, there are the annual bedding plants that have to be put in at the right time of year, then removed after their bloom times to make room for other annuals. Many offices, residences, and city streets go through this costly and time-consuming ritual several times a year. Currently, the flowers of choice are pansies, impatiens, and begonias, but a few years ago we were using marigolds, petunias, and portulaca. A switch was necessary because the predators and diseases the old bedding plants were prone to are now resistant to any poisons. Does this tell you something about planting too much of any good thing and then using too much poison?

Then there are the water-guzzlers—and these include everything from annuals and perennials to shrubs and ornamental trees to, of course, lawns. High-water-use TMT exotics vary from spot to spot. Azaleas are a disaster in Dallas, but drought tolerant in Atlanta. Aspens are weedy in Canada, but a struggle in Santa Fe. Generally, the dominant nursery stock for any one area is not quite drought-tolerant for that area. This is because gardeners have been trained to water, so they rot the roots of their suitable plants and get themselves stuck with plants that cannot live without supplemental water. Usually the only native plants used in an area are the flood-plain plants or the native shade trees.

Lastly, there are the exotics that are chemically dependent. They need regular doses of pre-emergents, artificial fertilizers, herbicides, fungicides, and pesticides to survive. These include hybrid tea roses, dahlias, and other plants that have been so horticulturally tampered with that they have lost their natural vigor, and any normally healthy plant that has been placed in an area that is too alien from its range of adaptation.

Of course, many TMT exotics fit into more than one of these categories. Frankly, I just don't see why we go to all that bother when there are much easier options available.

The Invasives   Don't panic, but we're being invaded by dangerous aliens. Not those drooling, metallic-looking creatures that Sigourney Weaver as the indomitable Ellen Ripley saved us from in those brilliant *Alien* movies. The aliens I'm referring to are plants. Exotic plants. And, make no mistake about it—these invasive exotics are noxious weeds, if the following definition has any merit: *A noxious weed is a plant alien to a geographical area whose presence threatens natural and agricultural ecosystems.* And like their science-fiction counterparts, these weeds are a major threat.

Take Florida. In the 1890s, a lady from that state visited the Louisiana Exposition and brought home a souvenir—a beautiful South American water hyacinth. She planted it in her water garden, and before long she was awash in this aquatic herb! It was taking over her entire backyard. So she pulled it up and dumped it into the St. Johns River, which ran behind her home. Today, Florida spends $9 million a year trying to keep water hyacinth from choking its rivers, canals, and lakes.

Invasive exotics are not new. They first came over on the *Mayflower*, in cattle feed. By 1672, twenty-two weeds were documented in New England, including the ubiquitous dandelion, which is native to northern Europe and Siberia. Today, invasive weeds are all over. Hundreds of them! And they're not just a nuisance, they're a real threat to our ecosystem—and our economy. A study by the Congressional Office of Technology

Assessment reported that between 1906 and 1991 invasive aliens (plants and animals) cost American industry, agriculture, and health services a cool $97 billion. Cornell University biologist David Pimentel calculates that the cost is now more like $122 billion a year.

The trouble is, most invasive weeds are attractive. They just don't look threatening. Incredibly, many are actually sold in nurseries as ornamentals. Brazilian pepper, for instance, was sold as a landscape plant in Florida and now infests over one hundred thousand acres of Everglades National Park. If they'd just stay put in the garden—the way other imported exotics do—they'd be

Water hyacinth *Eichhornia crassipes* is an aquatic herb, and one of the most costly invasives to control. Native to South America, it forms a solid mat on the water's surface, crowding out native vegetation and forming dense shade that changes water temperature and kills submerged plants. People in the Gulf states and central California think it's a contender for the title of Worst Weed in the World.

Crown vetch *Coronilla varia* is a low-growing perennial that is used commonly as a ground cover. That it does do—all too well! Native to Europe, southwest Asia, and northern Africa, this weed was introduced here in the 1950s for erosion control. It outcompetes natives, degrades wildlife habitats, and forms solid, single-species stands—monocultures! It's a pest from Canada down into the northeastern and midwestern states.

welcome. But they escape and naturalize and, because they lack the natural controls they had at home—insects, diseases, and grazers—they run amok. They often release toxins that poison our native plants. In their homelands, the other natives had thousands—even millions—of years to evolve immunities to these toxins. Our natives have not.

Take crown vetch—which comes from Europe, Asia, and North Africa. Driving along a highway in Canada recently, we saw mile after mile of this pink ground cover. I'm sure most people comment on how pretty it is. But what they're admiring is a monoculture—one plant that takes over, crowding out dozens of native species that *should* be grow-

Bluegum eucalyptus *Eucalyptus globulus* came to us from our friends Down Under. Many Californians think it's a native because it's been there approximately 130 years and is so widespread. It's very messy, littering the ground with shredded bark, small limbs, twigs, and leaves. The aromatic oil in its leaves makes it a fire hazard. California residents who saw the recent fires said that the whole tree would light in an instant like a torch. Bluegum eucalyptus spreads rapidly in grasslands and coastal scrub areas of California, displacing native flora and reducing biodiversity.

Russian olive *Elaeagnus angustifolia* has escaped cultivation in over seventeen states, from Canada down to Texas. It takes over streambeds, riverbanks, lakeshores, and wet meadows, choking out native cottonwoods and willows. Native to Eurasia, this tree has distinctive silvery gray leaves, woody thorns, and smooth reddish brown bark. It's popular for landscape use throughout the West.

ing there and destroying valuable wildlife habitats in the process.

In California, we've seen vast stands of Australian eucalyptus, with nothing but bare ground underneath. In the Southwest, roadsides are glutted with yellow sweet clover (doesn't even *sound* threatening!) from Eurasia. Along the Gulf Coast, Chinese tallow is a major problem, as is Mediterranean tamarisk in most western states. In the northeast, Norway maple, Japanese honeysuckle, and purple loosestrife are taking over, and bird's-foot trefoil, deliberately introduced from Europe as livestock fodder, is plaguing the Midwest. Florida, one of the worst-beleaguered states (along with Hawaii and

In the prairie states, in places where 150 species of native prairie grasses and flowers grew ten years ago, there is now only one species of noxious weed. When this happens, we lose irreplaceable genetic plant material, as well as the bees, butterflies, birds, and all

Tamarisk *Tamarix ramosissima, T. chinensis, T. parviflora*. There are several species of this small tree or tall shrub doing bad things in most of our western states. Tamarisks form dense, impenetrable tangles of stems up to thirty feet (9 m) tall, and inhabit riverbanks or areas where the roots can reach deep underground to suck desert springs dry, leaving rare Southwest species such as the desert pupfish, salamanders, and yellow-billed cuckoos without homes. Tamarisks are native to the Mediterranean and eastward through the Middle East to China and Japan. They were imported in the early 1800s as ornamentals, and are also used for erosion control. The food they produce is virtually useless to riparian wildlife.

Purple loosestrife *Lythrum salicara* is a perennial, and easily spotted because of its showy purple spikes. It's a native of Eurasia and colonizes meadows, marshes, riverbanks, and lakeshores. It can grow six to ten feet (180 to 300 cm) tall. Extensive stands of it displace native vegetation, threaten rare and endangered plant species, and reduce food supplies and shelter for wildlife. The only creatures that eat this plant are European beetles. As a result, this "purple plague" has overrun wetlands in forty-two states, from Maine to California, and put several species of amphibians and butterflies close to extinction. Some states have prohibited its sale. If you don't have any where you live, wait awhile; it's spreading its range.

California), is battling a long list of exotic weeds—many from Australia, including Queensland umbrella tree, Australian pine, and carrot tree. In Sharon Begley's piece "Aliens Invade America!" (*Newsweek* magazine, August 10, 1998), she reported that "The Australian melaleuca tree, introduced into south Florida in 1906 and planted as windbreaks and fence rows, has invaded half a million Everglades acres and was taking over an additional 50 acres [20 ha] every day."

the other creatures that depended on the diversity of the prairie for food and shelter.

We can see it happening. Where a multitude of flowers once bloomed in sequence over a seven-month period, there is now only one week of pretty color. In a pasture that supports a hundred head of cattle, a noxious inedible weed can crowd out all the forage and the rancher goes bankrupt. Noxious weeds outcompete row crops if the crops are not treated heavily with poisons—which eventually get passed on to us via our food. Some banks are now actually refusing loans to ranchers and farmers if they see evidence of noxious weeds on the land. Maybe this is ultimately our best weapon; people may not fight these weeds for environmental reasons, but they will when the problem hits them in the ol' wallet!

Landscaping Revolutionaries: Leslie Sauer and Andropogon Associates, Ltd.

When Leslie Sauer read the grade atop her term paper—a zero—she was bewildered. The paper was her final project for a course in plant ecology given by late ecologist Jack McCormick. "Was taking this course a mistake?" she wondered. It had nothing to do with her major—philosophy—and only came about because of a chance conversation with a professor of landscape architecture.

© Andropogon Associates, Ltd.

He had explained to her the phenomenon of succession—the systematic way that sequential plant communities evolve, diversify, and supplant each other over time. "That blew me away," she recalls. "I realized that this is how I look at the world."

When Leslie confronted McCormick, he explained that the zero represented "how much better the paper would have been if I had done it myself."

The term paper dealt with the environmental impact of a proposed jetport in central New Jersey, and McCormick submitted Sauer's paper to be read into the record of testimony the state legislature received on the jetport. A copy also went to the

Uncle Sam to
the Rescue? Ha!

So—if this situation is so serious, why doesn't our government do something? In spite of the fact that the federal government, under the leadership of Vice President Al Gore and Secretary of the Interior Bruce Babbitt, worked to bring this alien invasion out into the open in 1995, the government is a big part of the problem. Just one example: Federal agencies and state highway departments are handing out Siberian elm and Russian olive to ranchers in the Dakotas and Montana to be used as windbreaks. These trees now infest waterways from Canada down into Texas.

"An explosion in slow motion" is what New Mexico naturalist and rancher Robert G. Walton calls the spread of noxious weeds

---

governor. The jetport project never got off the ground.

Today, Sauer spends a good deal of time testifying at hearings and planning boards, and lectures corporate executives on the virtues of natural landscapes. A principal in Andropogon Associates, Ltd., a landscape architectural firm outside Philadelphia, Sauer and her partners are nationally respected pioneers in ecological landscape design.

The partners see their company as "a dream come true." They are a successful, creative business that does socially important work. The four principals are in fact two married couples: Leslie and her husband, Rolf E. Sauer, and Carol Levy Franklin and Colin J.

Franklin. Both men are also registered architects, and all four were good friends long before they formed their company in 1975.

The company's name comes from *Andropogon virginicus*, a common grass in the East that colonizes damaged landscapes and begins the environmental healing process. As Sauer puts it, the company's work involves "reweaving the fabric, putting the patterns of nature back in place."

Over the past decade, Andropogon has seen a growing client awareness and concern for environmental problems. "The consequences of piecemeal solutions and quick-fix approaches," says Sauer, "are now all too

apparent. Many of our clients have experienced adverse impacts on their own sites from the development of adjacent properties, and have been educated firsthand about the economic costs of ecologically inappropriate actions."

The market for their brand of landscape design has blossomed greatly since the company began; today their client list ranges from corporate giants such as Smith/ Kline Beecham to the City of New York, Yale University, and the U.S. Navy's Norfolk Naval Station. "The ideas are more mainstream now," says Sauer. "Their time has come."

State and federal government agencies have handed out highly invasive Russian olive and Siberian elm to ranchers in the Dakotas and Montana to be used as windbreaks. This has helped spread these trees from Canada down into Texas.

You'd think Uncle Sam might have learned from his fiasco with Asian kudzu. In the 1920s, the government promoted it for erosion control. Today kudzu is called "the vine that ate the South!"

over North America—leafy spurge, Russian knapweed, spotted knapweed, diffuse knapweed, Canada thistle, musk thistle, Scotch thistle, bull thistle, burdock, yellow toadflax (butter-and-eggs), poison hemlock, yellow starthistle, and houndstongue.

The weed seeds are spread in many ways. They wash down creeks and rivers and irrigation ditches. They are spread by highway departments when they mow rights-of-way. They are spread by road graders smoothing out dirt roads and the shoulders along highways. They travel in the mud under cars to home driveways. They are dispersed by wind and bird droppings. They infect hay fields and, when the hay is sold, the seeds go from farm to farm. Even our pristine wilderness is becoming weedy because horses spread the seeds along mountain riding trails, and off-road vehicles deposit seeds embedded in their tires.

Chapter 6

GETTING OFF THAT ARTIFICIAL LIFE-SUPPORT SYSTEM

"Nature's laws
affirm instead of
prohibit. If you
violate her laws,
you are your own
prosecuter, judge,
jury, and hangman."

Luther Burbank

A few years ago, I saw an ad for Home Depot that epitomizes the extent to which we willingly go for our typical American landscapes. The headline was a blatant call to arms: "Weekend warriors: prepare for battle." Below this the ad displays an impressive arsenal of lawn equipment, ranging from a rider mower designed to level tallgrass prairies to a chain saw that, presumably, will fell whatever trees on your property might be ruining the putting-green purity of your lawn.

The copy is also very revealing. It begins with the admonition, "It's Mother Nature versus you!" and ends by exhorting the reader to "show your yard this is one turf war you plan on winning." I have no doubt that the average American homeowner reading this ad did not find it frightening. Which, in itself, is frightening!

Contrast this with the native landscaper who can only shake his or her head in wonder at this attitude. Unlike the typical American landscape, upkeep in the natural or naturalistic landscape does not have to be drudgery—unpleasant chores that must be done regularly. Instead it can be pleasurable and creative, aimed not at mere survival, but at achieving aesthetic ends. Designs that mimic nature are, to a large extent, self-sufficient. Not maintenance-free, mind you. Left completely alone, a landscape, no matter how well planned and installed, soon becomes an overgrown weed patch. Or, as with a conventional landscape, which is on an artificial life-support system, it dies.

The naturalistic landscape requires pruning—just far less of it—and far less cleaning up because, as in nature, the dead leaves decompose and become compost, which in

turn becomes new soil. A tree stump becomes a home for wildlife. In a true natural landscape, you get a genuine sense of life going on all around you, over your head and beneath your feet. Conventional landscapes have that sterile, picked-up, ready-for-inspection look; they resemble true nature the way a submarine resembles a whale.

Upkeep Chores: A Comparison

As we mentioned previously, you can have a native landscape that is conventional in design—lawn, bedding plants, foundation plantings, etc.—and you'll be doing pretty much the same upkeep chores that you'd have with a traditional landscape. There'll just be a whole lot less of those chores.

But if you choose either the natural or naturalistic style (see Chapter 3), your landscape can have many different looks, depending on where you live, what plants are available, the size and topography of your property, and how much time and effort you want to invest getting it started and keeping it going. It's impossible to be specific about how much time you yourself would save going natural over typical; I know natural gardeners who spend a great deal of time—five hours or more per week—in their natural landscapes. Not because they have to, but because they enjoy it. Much of their work involves planting new things and expanding the garden or gardens.

Here, we're concerned only with performing those basic and necessary tasks that beset all homeowners: watering, mowing, edging, pruning, etc. The comparisons will be generally valid whether you live in the deserts of the Southwest or the forests of New England.

◆ **Mowing.** This is perhaps the most basic of maintenance chores. If you have conventional turf grass—Kentucky bluegrass, St. Augustine, fescue, bermudagrass—

This naturalistic landscape in Wisconsin— combining both indigenous and well- adapted exotics—requires a fraction of the maintenance time required for a conven- tional landscape. In a true natural land- scape you'll be able to measure upkeep in hours per _year_, not hours per _week_. How's that for a revolutionary idea?

you will mow one to three times per week, from spring through the summer, depending, of course, on where you live, the amount of rainfall you get, and your own personal tastes with regard to grass height. If you're an average homeowner and you use a professional lawn mainte- nance service, you're spending $761 annually. _With a native buffalograss lawn, you can mow one to two times per summer, depending on the variety of buf- falograss you use (some, like Prairie, grow to six to eight inches [15 to 20 cm] and pretty much stop there). That's an_ *attractive height to many people, so they don't mow at all. Eliminate all traces of lawn with a naturalistic or natural landscape, and the total time spent mowing is zip!*

Dethatching. Conventional lawns develop a thatch—a thick mat of unbiodegradable and impenetrable biomass that essentially prevents oxygen from getting down to the roots. This is very common, and is caused by lavishing too much fertilizer and too much water on the lawn. The grass gets overstimulated—it has far more energy than it needs, resulting in a buildup of plant tissues. Most warm-weather grasses have this tendency. Solution: buy a special mower—a vertical mower—designed to tear through this compacted biomass. Or, you can buy a dethatching attachment for your regular power mower. This requires you to remove the blade and put the attachment on—a ten-to-fifteen-minute operation. Or, you can buy a special rake designed for this job, and dethatch manually. *Or—you can use buffalograss, which requires no fertilizer and very little watering, and avoid the problem altogether.*

Bedding Plants. In a conventional landscape, you'll probably have lots of annuals—mums, pansies, you name it—taking up temporary residence in your garden. Temporary because they will have to be installed when they are at the beginning of their blooming period, removed when they peter out, and then replaced by something else that is colorful. This is as much fun as stoop labor on a tomato farm. *With a naturalistic landscape, the plants you put in become permanent residents. True, they won't be in bloom continually, but in nature, nothing is, and you don't expect that. Unlike those annuals, the natives will survive the cold season and come back the following year.*

Fertilizing. We've already mentioned one drawback to fertilizing—formation of thatches. Another is that it contributes to the contamination of our groundwater. Beyond that, applying fertilizers on your land requires time and effort—and money. Some fertilizer applicators can run as much as $600. But you get twenty

Lazy homeowner? Or environmentally responsible citizen? Leaving the leaves not only returns nutrients to the soil, it builds new rich soil.

different settings! *Now I'm going to let you in on a fabulous product that not only feeds and renews your soil, it helps rain soak into the soil better and helps retain moisture during the hot summer months. It covers your yard all winter and slowly decomposes so that, by spring, you'll have a marvelous all-natural composted mulch. Nobody is advertising this product, and you can't buy it at any garden center or nursery. Every fall you'll find masses of it there for the taking. I'm talking, of course, about leaves! We've got to stop thinking of fallen leaves as trash to be raked up, bagged, and hauled off to the landfill. The simple fact is, no matter what kind of landscape you have, you don't ever need commercial fertilizers; Mother Nature has provided you with an abundance of the natural kind—free.* By the way, when you calculate the time spent on maintaining the traditional landscape, don't forget the hours involved in raking up and bagging those leaves.

Edging. The typical American landscape is—or should be—militarily crisp, and that means periodically running up the driveway and along the sidewalks with an edger, either manual or power. Some people do this every third mowing. This eliminates the disturbing sight of errant blades of grass encroaching on the concrete. *Landscape revolutionaries, in case you haven't figured it out by now, are more informal and abhor straight lines and sharp edges, which are never found in nature.*

Burning. OK, there is *one* area of maintenance where going natural involves a task that you don't normally encounter in a conventional landscape: burning. In a re-created prairie landscape, or a woodland landscape with lots of low-growing understory, you might want to have a burn every two to three years. This may sound scary to you, but consider this:

nature uses periodic burns to revitalize the environment and the soil. Remember the big fires in Yellowstone National Park several years ago? The media were calling it a disaster, but naturalists knew better. Yellowstone came back healthier and more beautiful. We've seen successful burns in numerous home landscapes, from Texas up to Wisconsin—and they weren't on vast multi-acred properties. Before attempting one, notify your local fire department, tell them your intentions, and find out if there are any ordinances preventing this. They'll more than likely approve the burn and send someone out to oversee the operation, or give you a list of precautions. Also, don't forget to notify the neighbors so they'll know this is intentional. Pick a windless day and be sure to have water close at hand to keep things under control. If the grasses are dry, you shouldn't have any problem getting the fire started. Sometimes, however, you may resort to using old newspapers or kindling, just

Deb Harwell gives her half-acre property in a Milwaukee suburb a burn. The local fire department came out to make sure all was well.

the way you get your fireplace going. Grass, by the way, burns too quickly to create enough sustained heat to threaten your home.

◆ **Controlling Garden Pests.** We cover this in greater detail in Chapter 7. Here, it should suffice to say that, for most conventional gardeners, chemical warfare is an ongoing and accepted part of maintenance. Nibbled leaves and chomped-on blooms are the antithesis of the perfect traditional American landscape. *The landscaping revolutionary knows that there are plenty of natural remedies (predator insects) and preventatives (diversity of plant materials), so pest control is not a major concern.*

People kill wasps without realizing that they help control bagworms.

◆ **Watering.** This is probably not a major maintenance consideration for the average owner of a typical American landscape; coping with an automatic

© 1998 R. Crumb. Used with permission of Last Gasp of San Francisco.

sprinkler system—or, for those who do not have one, dragging out the garden hose and attaching the sprinkler attachment—is not an overwhelming calorie-burning chore. The main issue with watering is not the labor involved, but the amount of water that's consumed unnecessarily (see Chapter 2). *The native landscape is xeriscapic, and will require a fraction of the water expended on the conventional landscape.*

◆ **Pruning.** Homeowners with typical American landscapes tend to surround their homes with an assortment of crisply trimmed, razor-edged hedges, and topiaries in a wide and wild range of shapes—from simple "balls" and "mushroom caps" to leafy rabbits and elephants (see Chapter 8). This, of course, requires a steady hand, a good power or manual pruner—often several in different sizes—and the time and energy to engage in this "artistic" endeavor. Of course, the perfection of these creations does not last forever; branches and sprigs have an annoying way of growing at various rates, so the homeowner must go at it every few weeks to even things up. A moment's inattention and the shrubbery or hedge becomes lopsided or the verdant bunny rabbit may end the day sans an ear. *This sort of pruning is, of course, unthinkable in a natural or naturalistic landscape. Pruning is limited to the occasional elimination of a dead branch or two, and a little shaping to enhance rather than destroy the natural shape Mother Nature intended. The natural landscaper may spend two to four hours pruning all year, again depending on the size of the landscape and the number of plants requiring it.*

Chapter 7

ALTERNATIVES TO CHEMICAL WARFARE

"From the data that's out there, we could be looking at major biological problems in a generation or two."

Warren Porter
Zoologist, University of Wisconsin–Madison

I was driving to the store one afternoon when I spotted him. He was covered from head to toe in a bright yellow outfit that resembled the kind of gas-attack uniforms they issued to our troops during Desert Storm. He wore gloves, heavy rubber boots, and a face mask designed to filter the air he breathed. He held a hose attached to a tank on his truck, and he was busily spraying a tree.

I was impressed by the elaborate protective gear he wore—especially as he was spraying one of the least toxic pesticides used on landscapes—an oily coating that suffocates tree mites and other pests instead of poisoning them. And I couldn't help thinking about all those other professional applicators I've seen who spray pesticides and herbicides and fungicides, usually garbed in cutoffs, T-shirts, and sandals. No masks, no gloves, no nuthin' except their faith that what they were handling posed no danger to them despite what they did to the bugs and weeds.

While poring through my "toxics" file recently, I came across a ChemLawn sales brochure that I'd picked up at some home and garden show a few years back. In it, the company boasts about their safety precautions, such as protective clothing and periodic medical monitoring of employees, including lab tests for major organ functions. The company informs readers that they are working

What the well-dressed pesticide applicator should be wearing these days.

with the National Cancer Institute to determine what if any cancer risks are associated with long-term exposure to herbicides.

Now, hold on. Am I missing something? Don't all these precautions indicate that there are, in fact, risks associated with using their products? One of the last things they mention in this sales brochure is a warning that "people and pets stay off treated areas until the application has dried."

The Dark Side of 'Cides

According to data supplied by the EPA and the National Institute of Health, of the eighteen most commonly used herbicides, seven cause cancer, six cause birth defects, six cause reproductive defects, eight are neurotoxic, nine are damaging to the kidney and liver,

© "Off the Leash" by W. B. Park

© 1991 United Feature Syndicate, Inc

"Hi. Sign our no-insecticides agreement, and we'll stay clear of your house for a year."

and fourteen are irritants. Yet, in spite of this, Cindy Owsley, weed manager for Boulder County, Colorado, wrote an article for *Images*, the Boulder County Parks and Open Space publication, entitled "Why I Sprayed Herbicides on Earth Day." The title sounds like a sick joke! According to Jay Feldman, executive director of the National Coalition Against the Misuse of Pesticides (NCAMP), based in Washington, D.C., Owsley "seriously misled the public on critical questions of environmental safety. She is misinformed and, as a result, misinforms." Feldman adds that most herbicides can also be blamed for contaminating groundwater and poisoning fish, bees, and birds.

NCAMP is often smack in the middle of much of the controversy surrounding our use of toxic chemicals, and gets a lot of mail from people who currently or used to work in the pesticide business. Interestingly, these people choose to consult NCAMP about their concerns, rather than their employers or suppliers. For example, Larry Shaughnessy, in St. Peters, Missouri, wrote to say that he was

"worried about my health," and was afraid his exposure to Mosquitomist might be causing, among other problems, memory loss. NCAMP responded to Shaughnessy's letter by advising immediate medical treatment and pointed out that this chemical's active ingredient is chlorpyrifos, which has been shown to cause nausea, stomach cramps, headaches, and muscle twitching. It has also been linked, according to NCAMP, with peripheral neuropathy, altered brain-wave and sleep patterns, and behavorial changes. Chlorpyrifos, a DowElanco product, is the most widely used insecticide in the U.S. and has been linked to thousands of pesticide poisoning incidents. It is better known by a variety of trade names, including Dursban and Lorsban.

"Unfortunately," NCAMP added, "for applicators such as yourself, EPA allows far greater exposure and hazard than for the general public." However, the EPA now acknowledges that, overall, they have dramatically underestimated the hazards of multiple exposures to organophosphate pesticides.

Allen Tork, of Hastings, New Hampshire, wrote to say that pesticide advertising is very misleading. Once a certified applicator who had owned his own lawn care business, Tork said that "the chemical industry wants to give the public a false sense of safety about pesticides. One commercial," he says, "shows a man lying on the lawn using a bag of lawn chemical as a pillow. Another shows a teenager pushing a chemical spreader wearing shorts and sandals!"

Environmentalist Nathan Diegelman is also highly critical of these chemical companies. "Contrary to what lawn 'care' companies would like people to believe," he writes, "herbicides and pesticides are not magic bullets. They are broad-spectrum biocides, and by their very nature can harm organisms other than targeted species. This includes homeowners and their families, neighbors, pets, and all other forms of life. The pesticide industry downplays this by claiming their chemicals are heavily diluted, but doesn't mention the toxins are still extremely dangerous in small amounts."

In addition, Diegelman contends that the ingredients listed on the containers don't always tell the whole story. Many ingredients, he says, are classified as "inert," and so do not have to be listed. "But some of these so-called 'inert' ingredients," he warns, "such as benzene and xylene, are more toxic than the listed chemicals."

The simple fact is, lawn care chemicals are designed to destroy or control living organisms, so it's not surprising that when we are exposed to them there are health risks. We come in contact on our own property—or walking through a recently treated park or golf course. Exposure includes breathing in fumes, making direct contact with the skin, or, often long after the applications, when the chemicals have seeped down into our groundwater. A lady approached me one evening at a native plant conference and mentioned that she frequently jogged through a golf course near her home. "I don't run there for a few days after they spray," she said, "but when I return, I almost always find dead birds."

In a 1991 report to a Senate subcommittee on toxic substances, the U.S. General Accounting Office noted that one way to prevent public exposure to pesticides is to have commercial applicators notify neighbors seventy-two hours prior to lawn treatments. But, the report concluded, not all states require this, and among those that do, the notification programs vary widely in effectiveness.

The list of negative effects from our continuing use of chemicals—including over-the-counter household and garden pesticides—is staggering, and includes aggravating chronic respiratory diseases, nausea, dizziness, skin irritation, and damage to our endocrine and immune systems. In some cases, the damage is long-lasting and is passed on. According to a Colorado study published in the *American Journal of Public Health* (February 1995), children exposed to household pesticides

from birth to fourteen years old had a four-fold increase in the risk of soft-tissue sarcomas. One study showed that the highest incidents of birth defects occurred when one or both parents worked in the pesticide industry—manufacturing or spraying. The next highest category was people who were frequent and regular users of lawn chemicals.

Warren Porter, chair of the University of Wisconsin–Madison's zoology department, has been testing common pesticides on lab rats and was deeply troubled to find suppression of learning abilities and higher thyroid levels. "Some of these compounds can bioaccumulate in fat tissue," says Porter, meaning that members of each succeeding generation may receive an increasingly large dose from their parents in much the same way that interest compounds.

A Bad Solution to Our Population Explosion

Tests conducted by Dr. Theo Colborn, a staff scientist with the World Wildlife Fund, have convinced her that common chemicals used in and around American homes are causing dramatic reductions in male fertility and a growing number of deformities in the male anatomy. "I'm very worried," she says. "I think we have reached the point where there are measurable changes in humans and the environment from the chemical soup we carry around in us." These include fetal damage, testicular cancer, and penis distortions in newborn males.

Danish scientist Neils Skakkebaek reported that his fertility investigations, which involved fifteen thousand men in sixty-one separate studies, showed that sperm counts had declined 50 percent since the 1940s. Speaking at a congressional hearing in 1994, University of Florida researcher Louis Guillette told the assembled lawmakers, "Every man in this room is half the man his grandfather was." In all fairness, lawn chemicals are not solely to blame; there are numerous causes, including smoking, alcohol, sports injuries, and other lifestyle factors. Still, our constant exposure to everyday toxic chemicals is consistently put high up on the list by scientists and environmentalists who have studied the problem.

Part of the solution, Porter says, is to limit our use of chemical pesticides—especially the cosmetic use of chemicals to control lawn weeds. "Do we value dandelion-free lawns over our children?" he asks.

Fighting Back

The use of pesticides and other lawn chemicals, of course, goes on. According to the EPA, 21 million homeowners are annually applying over 25 million pounds of herbicides and 30 million pounds of pesticides to their residential lawns and gardens, and doing the applications themselves! The combined amount of pesticides used annually by untrained homeowners and professional applicators comes to 67 million pounds.

But we seem to be wising up. Fast. Among all those letters arriving at the offices of NCAMP are numerous requests for advice on how to stop municipal or utility company activities that may threaten the environment. A lady from North Strabane, Pennsylvania, wrote wanting to know how to fight a spraying program being implemented by her local power company to kill foliage under power lines. "Ours is a rural area," she wrote, "and many residents rely on well water. I'm worried about the effects."

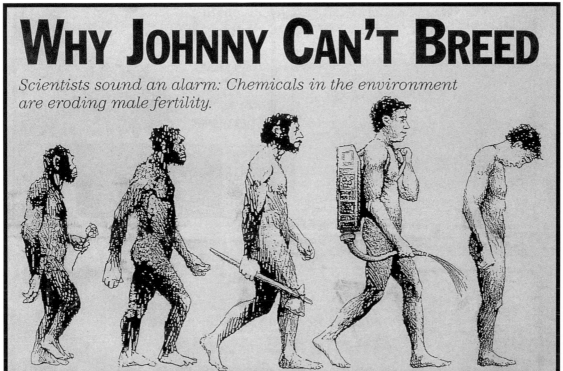

WHY JOHNNY CAN'T BREED

Scientists sound an alarm: Chemicals in the environment are eroding male fertility.

© Brian Reeves, originally published in *Isthmus*

Studies show that prolonged exposure to some pesticides can have adverse effects on our reproductive systems. There is no truth to the rumor that Planned Parenthood and Ortho are planning a merger.

Concerned citizens all over the country are taking action and making a difference. In May 1998, thanks to the combined efforts of parents, teachers, and environmental groups, the State of Maryland enacted a landmark school pesticide law that allows pesticide usage only "when other reasonable non-toxic means have been exhausted." It also treats exposure to pesticides as a public health issue, *expands notification guidelines beyond those advocated by the pesticide industry*, and gives adverse-effects information to parents of elementary school children before pesticides are used on school grounds. In Ohio, under NCAMP leadership, a local school district stopped using pesticides on all their grounds. In San Francisco, concerned citizens successfully had a broad pesticide notification law adopted. And in North Carolina, an agreement was reached with that state's utility companies to allow people living along rights-of-way to opt out of spraying programs, such as the one mentioned by the lady from Pennsylvania. These, and many other examples, show a significant shift in the public's understanding of pesticide dangers and a willingness to find and promote alternatives. Who says you can't beat City Hall?!

Pest Management

Garden pests are, to a large degree, a problem we've brought on ourselves. We like to mass plants, often of a single species, for visual effect. If a dozen mums are pretty, a hundred or more will really show those neighbors! But in doing this, we provide pests with a concentrated and easily accessible food source. With a handy food source, they reproduce more quickly. We till our soil, creating a hospitable environment for weed germination and growth. We even import pests from other parts of the world—intentionally and otherwise—but don't bring along the natural controls that kept them in check back home.

Ironically, we increase our pest problems by using the very pesticides that are supposed to be our salvation. While we're spraying the pests, we're also spraying the predator insects that could control them. Moreover, repeated use of pesticides tends to make them resistant to the poison, and we wind up with *superpests*! Which then require even stronger doses. And so on . . .

There is, however, a way out of this ridiculous cycle; it's called integrated pest management, or IPM, and it's an ecologically sound approach to pest control. It begins by remembering a favorite old axiom we all grew up on, "An ounce of prevention is worth a pound of cure." With the IPM approach, you use reasonable controls that start with preventative measures. This involves learning about the local pests, what they like, and when they are most likely to be a problem. IPM also involves coming to terms with how much damage to your garden is *too* much. Many environmental gardeners understand that a healthy garden is also a breeding, nesting, and feeding habitat for insects—most of whom are friendly—and so they allow a certain amount of nibbling.

IPM should be a balanced program, involving the use of pest-resistant plants, proper site selection, biological controls, and physical barriers. What it should *not* involve is the use of pesticides that can harm people or the environment.

You will want to look at techniques that will make your garden a lot less attractive to pests. These include planting **pest-resistant species** such as witch hazel and bayberry in the northeast; creosote, turpentine bush, and white thorn acacia in the Southwest; and gayfeather and autumn sunflower *Helianthus augustifolius* in the South. These all tend to have a fragrance or taste that insect pests find less than attractive.

Sunlight and good air circulation can reduce the need for fungicides on susceptible plants, and this can be accomplished by pruning and wider plant spacing.

Of all the insects in a typical garden, on average, only 1 percent can be called "pests." The other 99 percent are either benign or beneficial, such as these ladybugs.

By inspecting your garden regularly, you can spot potential problems early and abort their spread. **Remove dead or infected plant parts** and **handpick weeds and insect pests** before they multiply. You'll spend a lot less time doing this than fighting an infestation later.

Predators, such as birds and other insects, have been controlling pests long before we had all those commercial pesticides. If your garden has the kind of plants they like—such as nectar producers—they'll be there. Having a water source is helpful. Some predators—assassin bugs, ambush bugs, and soldier beetles—have wonderful names that tell you they are the hit men of the insect world. Many nurseries and garden centers now sell specific predators to combat specific problems: ladybird beetles (a.k.a. ladybugs) like aphids, mealy bugs, and other soft-bodied pests; lacewings feed on thrips, moth eggs, and scale; predatory mites eat spider-mites, thrips, and pollen; and praying mantises will eat just about anything, including other mantises.

But there is some question in the trade as to how effective these store-bought predators are compared to the predators that live naturally in your garden. Commercial ladybugs, for example, come primarily from California, where they are collected as they wake up from their winter hibernation. They are programmed to immediately fly high, where they are wafted all over the place by the winds. The ones you purchase may last two seconds in your garden and take off for another county! Praying mantises are voracious eaters, but if you buy non-natives (the green

ones), they'll gobble up both the garden pests and your native mantises (the brownish ones).

How Safe Is Safe?

Many people believe that a safe alternative to chemicals is **organic pesticides**. They do tend to break down into harmless substances soon after being applied. But this is misleading; in fact, many of the most toxic chemicals we know about occur naturally. Nicotine, for example, is a violent poison that attacks the human nervous system. Rotenone is extracted from the roots of many plants, and is moderately toxic to humans and many mammals, and highly toxic to fish and other aquatic life.

There was a time when I had difficulty photographing plants because I wanted leaves to be perfect—unnibbled. Later I realized that in nature this was next to impossible. Do you want perfect, but you don't want to use chemicals? They're doing great things with plastic these days.

There are insecticidal soap sprays on the market, which are absorbed through the cuticle covering the pest's body. Inside, they make cell membranes leaky, causing severe and lethal dehydration. The soap spray is effective only as long as it is wet. The trouble here is that some predator insects are also vulnerable. Often, a gentle hosing down of the infected plants with **soapy water** made with ordinary dishwashing liquid can be very effective against aphids and mites.

Some gardeners are enthusiastic about diatomaceous earth (DE) as a "safe" pesticide. Not actually a poison, it is a mineral that comes from the fossils of tiny plankton. Applied on or around plants as a superfine powder, DE absorbs the oil in an insect's cuticle covering the way sand or sawdust can absorb spilled motor oil. The insect then dies of desiccation. Slugs, snails, mites, cutworms, and moth larvae are most vulnerable, but so are some friendly predators. Also, while not toxic in the strictest sense, appliers are urged to wear face masks to avoid breathing the fine dust into their lungs.

You can also find strong advocates for a botanical pesticide made from the seeds of the neem tree. Neem is a repellent that is so powerful many leaf-eating insects give the entire plant a wide berth. It is said to be effective against over two hundred species of pests, including gypsy moths, whiteflies, and Japanese beetles. Neem has been deemed by the EPA to have an extremely low toxicity rating for humans and other mammals. It will not harm butterflies, honeybees, and ladybugs, and does not accumulate in soil or water.

The EPA has not evaluated the carcinogenicity of many widely used pesticides—another good reason to avoid their use. As Dr. Colborn says, "It's time for us to realize that when you dump something into the environment, you don't always know the consequences."

Chapter 8

HOMOGENIZE MILK, NOT LANDSCAPES

"All things have
their place,
Knew we how to
place them."

George Herbert
Seventeenth-Century Poet

Can you tell where these homes are located? Not by the landscapes, you can't. We've managed to clone the typical American landscape and turn our neighborhoods into Anywhere, USA. By the way, the answers are at the end of this chapter. No fair peeking.

Have you noticed? Something incredible seems to be happening to us. We're becoming standardized. Homogenized. Teenagers use the same hip jargon in South Carolina and South Dakota. The most popular TV shows in New Hampshire reflect viewing preferences in New Mexico. When we're on the road, we pass up local eateries in favor of nationally advertised fast foods. And when we spend the night, we prefer the predictability of motel chains to mom-and-pop inns. You can even stay at a Holiday Inn in Cracow, Poland!

Now, before you start wondering how a sociological treatise somehow blundered into a gardening book, let me quickly get to the point: nowhere is this cloning of America more apparent than in our own home landscapes.

The proof is right out your front door. Step outside and take a look at your landscape. Admit it, isn't it pretty much the same as all your neighbors'? Oh sure, you may have begonias where someone else has impatiens, but all in all, the look is pretty standard.

This is an "anywhere" look. And you can find it in neighborhood after neighborhood, from coast to coast.

You Are Not Alone!

In a program I've been giving around the country, I flash a series of slides showing home landscapes in various parts of the country—East Coast, West Coast, Midwest, Southwest, Dixie, even Canada. Only I don't tell the audience which is which. I let them guess. Nobody ever gets it right. The landscapes don't offer a clue because the same basic nursery stock is used all over. And most of it is exotics—from all around the world.

Once, Sally and I were walking in a neighborhood in another state, and I said, "What if you were blindfolded and magically wafted to this spot. Then the blindfold is removed, and this booming voice says, 'For a million dollars, tell me where in the country you are!' Could you do it?" She looked around and said, "I guess I'd lose a million dollars. I see plants from Asia, Africa, Australia . . . and not a single plant that's native to here."

That neighborhood, like virtually all American neighborhoods, had no sense of place. There had been no attempt to celebrate its regional uniqueness and special beauty. That's sad. And boring. That's also another reason to call these landscapes lemons.

In this chapter, we'll look at a few landscapes that do have a true sense of place. These examples are obviously attractive, and some have admittedly been designed and installed by professionals. But having a landscape with a sense of place does not necessarily require lots of money and horticultural skills; it's within the reach of anybody. Maybe these home landscapes will inspire you to convert your anywhere landscape to one that shows off your area's own plant palette. In Chapter 10 we'll talk about how to make that conversion as painless as possible.

Clearly, this is not New Jersey. This home in Scottsdale, Arizona, reflects the dramatic beauty of the Sonoran Desert. A majestic saguaro cactus and foothill paloverde are dominant, while color is provided by claret-cup cactus, Mexican evening primrose, Parry's penstemon, mountain marigold, and calylophus. The landscape was designed by Phil Hebets.

Landscape architect Sue Reed created this very appropriate woodland scene for her client in Amherst, Massachusetts. In this landscape, oaks and maples provide dappled shade for smaller dogwoods, witch hazels, and serviceberry trees. In the photo, we see flowering dogwood, mountain laurel, garden fothergilla, sweetfern, bloodroot, interrupted ferns, and Christmas ferns. In May and June, the garden is alive with color provided by foamflower, wild ginger, wild sarsaparilla, Canada mayflower, wild blue phlox, creeping phlox, sharp-lobed hepatica, and wild bleeding heart.

**The Wondra home outside Minneapolis
shows a prairie landscape composed of
both indigenous forbs and prairie grasses.**

**Johnny Mayronne, a landscape architect in
Covington, Louisiana, created this lovely
Gulf Coast landscape for his own home.
We're looking at the landscape in mid-
April, when the plant palette includes blue
phlox and yellowtop nestled in a mixture
of ferns. A red Florida anise is on the left,
with a younger white one on the right. The
pink shrub peeking through behind the
porch is Piedmont azalea.**

Cookie-Cutter Capitols

Of course, home landscapes aren't the only
ones lacking a sense of place. Virtually all
landscapes, from the sprawling grounds of
corporate headquarters to the small plots
around gas stations and fast-food empori-
ums, reflect the homogenized "anywhere"
look. But of all the places that *should* have a
native landscape—and for the most part
don't—I nominate our various state capitols.

When most people pay a visit to their
state capitol, they look around to spot a senator or maybe even the governor . . . and
sometimes they get lucky. But visitors who
expect to see landscapes with a sense of place
around their statehouse are almost always
out of luck. And I find this especially odd.
As native landscapes become more and more
popular across the country, the one place

you'd *expect* to see native vegetation is
around our state capitols. If for no other
reason than state pride: using native flora
is a great way to show off a part of what
makes each state special, even unique.

Instead, the typical capitol landscape is
amazingly predictable—lawns and mass
plantings of non-native mums, pansies,
hostas—plants from Europe, South America,
Asia . . . anywhere *but* the home state!

Admittedly, some do have a few natives
on the grounds, but these are usually venerable old trees that have graced the property for
many decades. And a few do allocate a portion of their grounds to a display of indigenous plants. The statehouse in Phoenix, for
example, has an attractive planting of
Sonoran Desert flora right in front of the
main entrance. Still, most of that landscape is
thirsty bermudagrass lawn.

The statehouse in Madison, Wisconsin, reflects not the flora of that state, but the misguided yet all too common idea that plants from anywhere else are better than native flora. Moreover, the exotic bedding plants are mostly annuals, and need to be replaced regularly.

Notice, I'm not saying these landscapes are unattractive. Many are very attractive. But that's not the point. The vast majority of these landscapes have little or nothing to do with the native flora *of* those states. According to Mona Robison of the California Native Plant Society, the landscaping at their state capitol in Sacramento is a "hodgepodge" of specimen trees from all over the world. And in Baton Rouge, Chinese tallow graces the capitol grounds— that's a very invasive alien tree that is already destroying ecosystems in Louisiana.

Iowa and Nebraska are prairie states, but do the statehouses in Des Moines and Lincoln reflect their tallgrass prairie heritage? Not unless a Kentucky bluegrass lawn is your

idea of prairie. Why not have restored tallgrass prairies around those capitols? The combination of native grasses and prairie flowers would be spectacular. Not to mention that since 99.9 percent of our prairies have been plowed under or developed over, the state governments would be making an important environmental statement by restoring some of it. It would also be a fiscally responsible statement; once it's established, the prairie could survive on rainfall alone. And, it would eliminate all that mowing and upkeep.

Which brings up another issue: most of these capitol landscapes are high-maintenance and costly, and the state's taxpayers foot the bill. Each year, according to

Nebraska is a prairie state, but the grounds of the state capitol in Lincoln reflect none of this heritage. That's a shame, because a restored tallgrass prairie would not only be attractive and educationally valuable—once established, it would also cut way down on maintenance costs.

The Arizona Capitol in Phoenix is surrounded by six and a half acres (2.6 ha) of grounds, most of which are devoted to non-native lawn and trees that need irrigation to survive the brutal Arizona summer. But at the front entrance is a tribute to the Sonoran Desert—a cactus garden containing saguaro and other native cacti.

an article in the *Richmond Times-Dispatch*, the grounds crew at the Virginia state capitol, among other chores, plants nine thousand tulip bulbs and two thousand pansies, spreads a ton of grass seed and four tons of fertilizer, and trucks away twenty tons of leaves—which, if left, would rebuild the soil and make all that fertilizer unnecessary. The article also mentioned that plans are afoot to redesign that landscape. My fingers are crossed. Virginia is a beautiful state with beautiful native flora, and I can only hope that they'll take this opportunity to show the other states how to do it right!

The New Mexico state capitol in Santa Fe greets visitors with a display of Bradford pears—a hybridized fruitless trash tree! Gladiolas and other non-natives line the walk, while the building is ringed by highly invasive Russian olive. Boy, that sure says "New Mexico" to me!

Landscaping Revolutionary: Darrel Morrison, FASLA, and Dean of Environmental Design at the University of Georgia

There's a familiar old saying: "Those that can, do; those that can't, teach!" And then there's Professor Darrel Morrison, who is both an outstanding landscape architect and one of the most influential teachers in the country.

As with most truly creative people, Morrison is unconventional. A favorite, and true, anecdote repeated by his protégés and colleagues involves his role as site planner for the National Wildflower Research Center outside Austin, Texas—a project that involved him for three years. Not content to stay at a local hotel during his frequent trips to Texas, and visit the site during normal working hours, Morrison showed up with a sleeping bag and camped out on the land. "It's important to experience the evening sights and sounds," he explains. "And the light quality, especially at sunrise and sunset."

During these quiet times, he made countless

sketches of the natural landscape and came to understand the terrain in an intimate way that greatly influenced not just his own approach to the designs, but the attitudes of those working with him. Richard Archer, one of the architects on the project, said of Morrison's unique approach, "We developed an attitude toward the buildings and

grounds before we began drawing. It took on a life of its own."

Rare among landscape architects, Morrison is highly knowledgeable about the native plants that are his stock in trade. More importantly, he understands how individual plants function in harmony with their environment—the natural plant community. For Morrison, a landscape is not simply a pleasing assortment of colors and textures, it is the harmonious interplay between plant species and the soil, available water, and wildlife that compose the site.

Asked to describe his approach to his work, Morrison tells of the time Louise Allen, a respected leader in Atlanta's gardening community, was watching him oversee the installation of one of his designs. "You know, Darrel," she said, "this may be controversial. I certainly hope so!"

A Yaupon Holly Is Not a Lollipop

Give me a dollar for every yaupon holly, abelia, Japanese boxwood, or dwarf burford that's been pruned into a little French poodle, a giant gumdrop, or a lollipop, and I could finance Donald Trump's next three projects.

The curious practice of taking perfectly innocent shrubs and ornamental trees and carving them into an infinite array of forms—from the purely geometric to the whimsical to the downright silly—is called topiary. Some call it an art form. If so, I'd put it closer to ice sculpture than Rodin. But that's just me.

In 1712, Dezallier D'Argenville wrote, in his *The Theory and Practice of Gardening*, "This topiary is the richest and most distinguished in the whole business of gardening." Author Barbara Gallup calls it "enchanting." On the other hand, nineteenth-century architect William Robinson referred to it as "graceless and inert," and Dallas landscape architect Michael Parkey calls it nothing less than "plant abuse" and says that it should be punished by sending the perpetrators to an incompetent barber. Clearly, there seems to be little in the way of ambiguity when the topic is topiary.

No matter how you feel about topiary, you have Cnaius Matius to thank (or blame) for it. A close buddy of Julius Caesar, Cnaius was credited by Pliny the Elder with having invented topiary during the first century B.C. It quickly caught on with the trendsetters of the day, and became de rigueur at every fashionable Roman estate.

Topiary received a new spurt of popularity during the Italian Renaissance. Folks lacked a wide range of plant materials in those days, so if they wanted variety in their garden, they had to achieve it with clippers and a fertile imagination.

Topiary arrived on these shores around 1690, with geometric forms appearing in many Williamsburg gardens. Today, some of the most extravagant examples are still on the East Coast, with Longwood Gardens in Pennsylvania and Callaway Gardens in Georgia looking not unlike botanical Disneylands.

Perhaps topiary reached its peak of popularity in eighteenth-century England when, according to gardening author Miles Hadfield, "Englishmen, confident in man's innate superiority over the natural world, decided to accept it as an ally with whom they could play." Topiary, says Hadfield, is a style of gardening "which violently defies nature to show man's domination of it."

Of course, no matter how you personally view topiary, two things are irrefutable: One, topiary is a heck of a lot of work, whether you do it yourself or pay to have it done.

This is a yaupon holly.

These are lollipops.

This is a yaupon trying to look like lollipops.

And, two, it is definitely *not* what Mother Nature had in mind.

Here are a few other examples of topiary I have come across in my travels:

Ziggurat? Or a Dairy Queen dip cone?

Found in Los Angeles—*before* the earthquake.

Maybe the owners saw one too many grain silos?

Spotted on a drive along the oceanfront—big surprise.

Bowling ball? Meatball? The fourth moon of the planet Morfutz?

Split personality—natural on top and topiary on the bottom!

No, it's not a "box" elder.

I don't have a clue . . .

A Lollipop Is Not Forever   Let's say you own some topiary, but don't want it anymore. Maybe you inherited it when you bought your house, along with the roaches and the crack in the patio. What can you do to convert your lollipop back into the beautiful ornamental it was intended to be? Here's a sure-fire topiary restoration plan:

1. You'll need two pruners: a long-handled pair about two feet (60 cm) long, and a smaller one-handled pruner, about nine inches (25 cm) long.
2. Now, check the trunks. If two are growing into each other and are rubbing off the bark (providing an opening for infection), keep the trunk that is growing outward, and remove the one that is growing inward. Cut it back to ground level.
3. Check the aesthetic quality of the trunks that are left. Be very cautious about taking out trunks that are not potential problems. Have someone pull the trunk in question as far out of the way as possible, so you can see how the tree will look without it. If you're still in doubt, leave it. You can always remove it later, but you can't glue it back.
4. Now, start cutting off all the branches that grow in toward the center of the tree. Cut every one of them off at the collar—that's the slight thickening of the branch where it joins a larger branch or trunk. The idea here is to give the tree a nice, airy, open feel in the middle.
5. If the branches have been hedged or hacked back so many times that the branching looks like a starburst of mini-branches (a very ugly look), cut back to the first long, undamaged branch that points outward.
6. Do not cut off the end of a branch for at least five years; this allows the branches to grow long enough to give your yaupon, or whatever, a treelike structure. After five

years, if your tree is as large as you want, you can begin cutting off end branches—but *always* cut them off at a collar. Do not just snip off the end.

Most evergreen shrubs and trees can be safely pruned at any time of year, but be cautious about pruning too close to the first cold snap of the year. You'll stimulate new growth that might be snuffed out. Also, never paint the cuts. They'll gray over very quickly, protecting the tree from disease.

Because we're an immediate-gratification society, you'll be pleasantly surprised when you see how much better your untopiaried tree will look right away. Give it a month or two, and it will look even better. If only your topiaried evergreen knew you were reading this, it would sigh with relief, knowing that its embarrassing days as a lollipop were coming to an end.

Answers to Quiz

Maryland
Arizona
Ontario, Canada
Iowa

The topiary display at Longwood Gardens in Kennett Square, Pennsylvania, is a popular tourist attraction. Fifty-five separate examples of topiary occupy the garden—less than an acre (.4 ha) in size—and require 325 man-hours of pruning annually to look their snappiest.

Chapter 9

WHERE HAVE ALL THE FIREFLIES GONE?

"In wilderness is
the preservation
of the world."

Henry David Thoreau

We may be on some sort of a halting journey toward
understanding the world, and ourselves within it, as
one system.

Thomas J. Lyon
This Incomperable Lande

One of the genuine rewards of writing our books (it sure ain't the money!) is the many friendships Sally and I have made in our travels. While we were working on *Gardening with Native Plants of the South*, we met and immediately bonded with Kitty and Neil Taylor in Colliersville, Tennessee. One night, after dinner at their home, Kitty, a talented landscape designer, suddenly announced, "Now we're going out for a special treat." We had no idea what she meant, but we followed along, intrigued.

The four of us tromped across several large pastures (they also raise horses) and finally stopped at what looked like a giant hedgerow. It was very dark—the moon was hidden behind a cloud—and so far we hadn't seen anything to warrant her enthusiasm. "Follow me," she said, and led us through an opening in the hedgerow into yet another large field.

Sally and I stopped in our tracks and stared. Then we started grinning and laughing giddily, like kids confronting a mountain of brightly wrapped packages beneath the Christmas tree. What we were seeing that night was to our minds even more beautiful—and certainly more rare. We were looking at the blinking lights of *a billion fireflies*—a galaxy of them—rising nine or ten feet (270 to 300 cm) off the ground. They were swarming in all directions at once, and we were quickly engulfed by them.

I tried to remember the last time I'd seen a gathering of fireflies. Never mind a billion—maybe just a dozen or so. Not for a very long time. As a kid, I used to see hundreds of them darting about on a summer's night. Not out in the woods or in a public garden, but right around my suburban lawn-centered home. My friends and I would chase them and capture them in jars, and then place the jars next to our beds so we could enjoy the soft illumination as we fell asleep. If you're of a certain age, I'll bet you did, too.

Our firefly population has diminished over the years, and most of us probably never notice until one day we spot a solitary firefly meandering about in someone's yard and we realize, hey, something's wrong. I used to see swarms of them. Come to think of it, there used to be lots more songbirds around, too. . . .

Our Bird-Brained Approach to Birds

We've been less than perfect stewards of our world. Let's face it, we're *us* centered. We build for us. We clear the land for us. We pour pollutants into rivers and lakes and oceans in the process of making things for us. And we give little thought to the fact that we are not alone on this planet, that everything we do has consequences.

I believe it's true that we're becoming more environmentally aware these days—at least if bumper stickers are any indication. We've all seen the ones urging us to "Save the Whale" and "Save the Tiger." But what we don't see are bumper stickers urging us to "Save the Anole" or "Save the Bluejay." Our environmental awareness all too often extends only to the familiar and the cute and cuddly. (I'd love to see a bumper sticker saying, "Save the Sampson's Pearly Mussel.")

According to monitoring organizations such as the Breeding Bird Survey, which has been counting our feathered friends along three thousand survey routes in the U.S. and Canada since 1966, segments of our native bird population have declined dramatically over the years. Some, such as warblers, vireos, flycatchers, and thrushes, have declined by 50 percent or more in the past few decades. Some bird populations remain stable for the time being, and some have increasing populations. But significantly, it's in the urban and suburban areas where the most precipitous declines have been noted.

There are many reasons: attacks by non-native predators such as the European starling, North American cowbirds that lay their

Two hundred years ago, North America (including Hawaii and Puerto Rico) was home to approximately 700 species of birds. Today, 33 are extinct, 80 are classified as endangered, and over 150 are in trouble in all or parts of their ranges. Many others, according to the National Audubon Society, are in apparent decline.

eggs in other nests, avian viruses that are spread from bird to bird through droppings in outside commercial feeders, pesticides, and cats. While family cats certainly contribute to the carnage (our own Felix and Fanny did quite a number on visiting hummingbirds this past summer, despite the fact that we'd placed the feeders high enough to keep our athletic felines from nabbing them in flight), it's feral cats—house cats that are abandoned in the wild and left to fend for themselves—that are far more destructive to the bird population.

But, according to Vincent Muehter, associate director of conservation for the National Audubon Society, "the number one reason for the declining bird population is *habitat degradation*." Without reckoning the cost, we've destroyed wildlife habitats and eliminated migratory routes. A woodland is leveled to make room for a housing development—and the developers and the people

who will live there are unaware of the irony that it already *was* a housing development for numerous bird species, as well as other critters.

Pollinators—hummingbirds, bees, bats, butterflies, and moths—are also declining in great numbers around the world. These creatures perhaps best exemplify the intricate and harmonious interconnectedness of the natural world—plants and animals that could not go on without each other. As authors Stephen Buchmann and Gary Paul Nabhan point out in their book, *The Forgotten Pollinators*, human-induced changes in pollinator populations can have a domino effect, leading to a "cascade of linked extinctions" of dissimilar species.

Many people really don't see why all this talk about species extinction is such a big deal. After all, they tell you, we've been losing species all along. They tell you that, here in the U.S., we lost the passenger pigeon and the Carolina parakeet, and our daily lives don't seem to be any the worse for it. The dodo, the great auk, the Labrador duck, and the ivory-billed woodpecker are now all gone, they point out, and still we go on our merry way. And when the brouhaha erupted in the Pacific Northwest over cutting down old-growth forests versus saving the spotted owl, they argued that lumberjacks with big families and bigger bills to pay were more important and they had no hesitation in siding against the little raptor.

Radio talk-show host Michael Reagan once told a listener that "environmentalists care more about squirrels than they do about people." What rubbish! What Reagan and far too many others don't grasp is that environmentalism is about preserving a proper balance between us and the natural world around us—plants and animals alike. It's like it says in that TV commercial for the cotton industry where the little schoolkids are on a field trip to the big city with their teacher. As they cross the street they all hold hands and the voice-over says, "What's the first thing we learn? That if we don't all get there together, we won't get there at all."

The issue isn't that we're losing species, it's that we're losing species *so quickly.* Living species of plants and animals are disappearing around the world *one thousand times faster* than at any time in the past 65 million years. Harvard's E. O. Wilson calls this "The largest spasm of extinction since the dinosaurs vanished."

And, according to the *Red List of Threatened Plants* (published in 1997 by the World Conservation Monitoring Centre), the United States has a larger percentage of endangered plant species than 233 other countries, with Hawaii, Florida, and Texas being the three most severely affected states. We rank fourth in terms of species at risk with 29 percent of our native species—4,669 specific species—endangered. And if you guess that China and Brazil are worse off than we are, you'd be wrong. Topping the list are St. Helena, Mauritius, and Seychelles—all small island countries.

We lose sight of the fact that we are part of an elaborate tapestry, a wonderfully intricate synergistic community where everyone and everything plays a part. We don't always know exactly what part—and how vital it may be—that every plant or animal plays, but consider this scenario:

Imagine that you're on an airplane flying several miles up. There's a lunatic on board who is running around the plane with a pair of pliers, pulling out rivets. He pulls out quite a few, and a number of passengers (a minority) voice concern—some are even alarmed. But the majority think, "Everything appears to be OK. The plane is still aloft, and the flight attendants are beginning to serve cocktails, so why can't those alarmists on board just shut up and enjoy the ride?" Ultimately, of course, the madman will pull out one rivet too many, and the plane will fall apart.

Now imagine that those rivets are animal and plant species. How many can we afford to lose before it all falls apart?

This delightful creature is an anole *Anolis carolinensis*, and is found in the southeastern U.S. It's often incorrectly called the American chameleon. In fact, it's not related to the chameleon family. It grows six to eight inches (15 to 20 cm) long and can turn colors depending on what it's sitting (standing?) on—from green to yellow to brown or gray, or a mix. The males have a pink throat sac that inflates when they're in the mating mood.

Giving Something Back

So, you ask, what has all this got to do with gardening?

Just this: we have all become aware—some more reluctantly than others—about all the environmental woes besetting our planet. Everything from global warming to depletion of our ozone layer, from acid rain to contaminated wetlands, from disappearing rain forests to eroding topsoil. Often, the language surrounding these issues is highly tech-

Habitat loss is by far the biggest cause of wildlife decline.

nical and arcane, and we feel overwhelmed and intimidated. We're just average folks trying to get along; what can we do about such immense problems? The temptation is just to sit back and say, let the government handle it. Leave it up to the scientists. Leave it in the hands of Providence.

In fact, we can do a lot as individuals, and we can start right in our own front and back yards. The typical American landscape is not, as a rule, wildlife friendly. Shrubs are clipped into tight impenetrable masses that discourage nest building, many exotics do not provide the food that native wildlife is used to, the ground is compacted and dead, lacking earthworms and other protein sources for birds, and vast lawn areas do not provide shelter from predators. By changing the way we landscape our homes—by seeing our landscapes from a bird's or butterfly's perspective—we can give them safe places to breed, feed, lay eggs, and grow to maturity.

As garden writer Michael Pollan points out, "Most of us automatically assume that the best we can do in nature is the least: to

The Texas Parks and Wildlife Department encourages landscaping that attracts and shelters wildlife, even in urban areas. Their biologists are now training volunteers in an outreach program modeled after the one created by Master Gardeners. By following the program's guidelines, homeowners can have their properties designated official Texas Wildscapes. Similar programs are offered by the Wild Ones and the National Wildlife Federation.

leave the land alone. Yet as many a gardener has observed, it is possible to make changes . . . that actually contribute to its ecological health—that add to the abundance and diversity of life in a place."

That, in a nutshell, is the essence of natural landscaping. For a very long time now we've been taking with both hands. Now it's high time we started giving something back to the creatures with whom we share the planet. And, by the way, if you have a larger than average property, don't limit your thinking to just birds and butterflies. While they are not always ideal in small suburban and urban areas, raccoons, opossums, and other small (and safe) mammals can be wonderful neighbors in more rural settings.

Imagine a neighborhood where a portion of every yard—perhaps where the backyards join—is in a natural state. Shade trees provide not only nesting places, but an elaborate buffet for woodpeckers and other birds. Understory—all those low-growing plants that are usually cleared out beneath the shade trees—would provide lush shelter for small mammals. And wildflowers would attract the pollinators that are so vital to our own survival. And, of course, the plants would be indigenous to the site. Why is this so important? Wouldn't any number of well-adapted plants do as well? In some cases, yes. In some cases, uh uh!

Solve One Problem, Create a Bigger One

The trouble is, we rarely know what we're doing when we import and use exotic species. I mentioned earlier the European starling, which was imported simply because it was pretty, but has turned into a menace to native songbirds. This happens in the plant kingdom as well.

Author Sara Stein tells a story about the plight of the native dogwoods *Cornus florida* in her area of New York State. Seems that a Chinese dogwood *Cornus kousa* was imported into the local nursery trade and quickly became very popular. No question about it, the import was a beautiful tree, with showier blooms and larger fruits. And so the native dogwood lost favor, and became little used in home landscapes. This, of course, had a negative effect on the local bird population, which counts on the native dogwood as a food source. The Chinese dogwood doesn't do them any good because the fruits are too sweet—more like dessert than the hearty meal they need to build body fat for their fall migration. Moreover, the fruits of the Chinese dogwood are too large for the birds to easily eat them. In China they're eaten by monkeys. And there are precious few monkeys running wild in New York State.

Plant It and They Will Come

The first step in creating such a habitat garden is to do a survey of the wildlife in and around your neighborhood. Observe how they live and where and on what. Get a good regional field guide to help you identify the critters you want to see in your yard. But, as Marcus Schneck points out in his *Butterflies: How to Identify and Attract Them to Your Garden*, "While guides . . . are helpful in identifying butterfly species and describing their general ranges, nothing can compare to direct observation of what is happening naturally." For example, a guide may recommend a certain plant for attracting a specific butterfly species, but the plant may be a generalized suggestion and may not grow in your part of the country.

The key to a successful wildlife garden is simple: give them what they want . . . and the wildlife will show up. Look, if your lovable (and rich) old Uncle Henry were coming for an extended visit, you'd do everything you could to make his stay as pleasant as possible. If he prefers decaf coffee, you'd stock up. If he loves *Jeopardy*, you'd put a TV in his room. If he has a thing for Middle Eastern food, you'd learn to make falafel and hummus.

Same with the critters. They have specific requirements, too. And, because you'll want a diverse selection of wildlife, you'll want to plant a diverse array of vegetation. Here are just a few suggestions for creating a successful wildlife garden:

- Sunny areas should have nectar-rich wildflowers for butterflies, hummingbirds, and bees. Use lots of tubular red and purple flowers and lots of sunflowers, asters, and daisies, or a good regional wildflower mix.

- Also in sunny areas, plant regionally appropriate female shrubs and ornamental trees for winter and spring migration fruits, such as possumhaw, wax myrtle, yaupon holly, toyon, or Baja California bird bush. For fall migration fruits, plant hawthorn, dogwood, persimmon, sumac, or a fruit tree that you may wish to share with the wildlife . . . assuming you're fast enough.

- In shady areas, include evergreens and thicket shrubs for hiding, sleeping, and nesting. Add a shade-tolerant bird-fruit tree such as Carolina buckthorn or viburnum. Use nutritious ground covers such as Turk's cap, pigeonberry, or inland seaoat.

- Color is a major factor in attracting butterflies. Some favor specific colors and will bypass other bright colors. Some prefer orange, while others opt for reds. Provide a range of options for them, including white, purple, yellow, pink, and true blues.

- Hummingbirds and butterflies are also partial to flowers with specific shapes. Hummers like funneled or cone-shaped blooms (their thin long beaks tell you that), and trumpet-shaped morning glories are big favorites with butterflies such as long-tongued swallowtails and fritillaries.

- Make sure there are safe places for spiders to build their webs, birds to build their nests, and caterpillars to begin their wondrous metamorphosis.

- Put in a small water feature or bird bath—but out in the open so cats and other predators can't hide within pouncing range.

- If feasible, allow some ground to remain bare near the water feature. Damp earth can be a gathering place for male butterflies in a practice called "puddling."

A good wildlife garden will provide safe nesting places for birds, out of the wind and direct sun.

Who says you have to have a natural landscape to attract wildlife?

- Because the planet rotates, different parts of the garden will change from sun to shade at various times of the day. Not all species of butterflies take nectar at the same time, so keep this in mind when planting.
- Don't introduce exotic larvae or chrysalids to your garden—they will die.
- Put in or leave a piece of dead wood, or a tree trunk. This is habitat for many critters, such as grubs and lizards, that are an important part of the ecosystem.
- Never use pesticides.

Wild Gardens and Wilder Beasties?

When the subject of wildlife gardens comes up, invariably the concomitant subject of undesirable critters follows. "I'm all for butterflies and songbirds," people say, "but I don't want deer and rabbits and raccoons—and even *worse* invading my yard!" This is not an uncommon concern. Browsers have decimated more than a few gardens, and methods of discouraging them are numerous and of questionable efficacy. Some of the preventative measures currently in vogue include spreading human hair (harvested from the local barber shop) around the garden, and running low-voltage wires around the yard. There's even a product called Zoo-Doo, which is composed of the feces of carnivores (collected from zoos), that is also supposed to be effective. Motion-detection lights and stringing tin cans around the garden have also been tried. Fences, of course, seem the most logical solution to keeping hungry critters at bay, but all too often they are jumped over or burrowed under. Anyway, who wants a six-foot (180-cm) deer fence around their suburban front or back yard.

There is ample evidence that homeowners inadvertently invite browsers and other creatures onto their property in more ways than by how they landscape. If you feed your pets outdoors and they don't belong to the clean-plate club, other animals will show up to polish off what Fifi and Muffy left behind. Uncovered or easily accessible garbage cans are also irresistible.

The thing is, you don't have to have a natural landscape to be visited by animals. Deer, foxes, skunks, and opossums are not uncommon sights in suburban neighborhoods where there isn't a single natural landscape for miles. Sally and I went to New Jersey for my high school reunion several years ago, and as we drove up to our friends' home where we would be staying, we saw five adult white-tailed deer crossing their well-manicured suburban lawn. To appreciate the irony of this, know that Sally and I have lived in the mountains of northern New Mexico for several years now, and we have yet to see a single deer. We know they're around because we see their tracks. In the forests around our home, the deer still have room—at least for

the time being—and are not forced to find dinner on our land. In New Jersey, they have been squeezed out of their remaining habitats and must boldly forage anywhere they can out of sheer desperation. Wouldn't you?

Many people complain about the "invasion" of so-called unwanted wildlife into their neighborhoods. But like almost everything else in the world, this is a matter of perspective. Many others see this "problem" as having more to do with our own overbreeding than with theirs. It isn't that the animals

The transformation of a caterpillar into a magnificent butterfly is one of nature's greatest feats. How many youngsters even know this sort of thing is going on?

are invading us, we're invading them. As our numbers grow, we must move farther and farther out into undeveloped areas, putting up new homes, shopping malls, schools, churches, office complexes, and industrial parks, and in doing so we leave the creatures less and less habitat. We take the attitude that we're more important than wildlife; we have a right to go wherever we want. Ask any Native American how that works.

Lions, Coyotes, and Bears, oh My!

So let's say you're tolerant of browsers, and you're committed to peaceful coexistence. You even willingly sacrifice a portion of your plantings to them, and run for your camera—not the shotgun—when you spot some on your property. But, there's a limit, right? What about that other category of wildlife? Predators!

Even environmentally conscious citizens voice concerns about coyotes, foxes, bears, etc., and fear that they'll become more than a nuisance. After all, cougars have been seen meandering through school yards, apartment complexes, and even shopping malls!

Mark and Sarah Squire, of Colorado Springs, Colorado, have a naturalistic land-scape—wild grasses, wildflowers, and other native plants—and are enthusiastic about their "naturescape." Still, they were presented in a *Wall Street Journal* article as being fearful for their children when they spotted coyotes around the sandbox on their property. "If coyotes can take down a cow," Sarah was quoted as saying, "they can take down a three-year-old."

Well, yes . . . if true. But the fact is, according to Brooks Sahy, executive director of the Predator Defense Institute in Eugene, Oregon, "Ninety percent of a coyote's diet is rodents. They don't go after cows, singly or in packs." The vast majority of these concerns, he adds, have more to do with what

people imagine might happen than what would or could happen. Most wildlife don't want to have anything to do with us. The other fact you need to know is that Sarah Squire *never said that*. Much of what we read and hear about wildlife "invasions" in the popular media is exaggerated nonsense, the result of plain ignorance. (In Chapter 13, I'll go into more detail about this *Wall Street Journal* article that presented such a distorted view of nature.)

Ultimately, people who choose to live in rural areas must expect to encounter wildlife of every kind. If they are skittish about this, and view with alarm any animal more feral than their domesticated dog, they have two choices: they can move back to the big city and live in a high-rise condo (where they can then worry about confronting other preda-tors—the ones who carry switchblades and Saturday night specials), or they can make the effort to learn about the wildlife in their region, and come to understand the realities and beauty of coexisting with them in this environment. They might even find it rewarding.

Trade Frisbees for Fireflies

One last word: People have said to me on more than one occasion, "I can't convert my lawn into a wildlife garden. Where would my children play?" At the risk of sounding sim-plistic, how about—in the wildlife garden? What better gift can you give your kids than an opportunity to experience nature "up close and personal." Can you really compare tossing a Frisbee to the joy of seeing a mother bird feed her young? Or watching a spider spin a web? Or, yes, spotting a red fox scurrying across your property followed by her kits? The real issue is giving our young-sters an option to sitting inside playing com-puter games! For other people's thoughts on this, read Chapter 13, "Who's Afraid of Virginia Creeper?"

Chapter 10

CONVERTING YOUR YARD . . .
AND YOUR NEIGHBORS

"You get used to
the overall look of
a wild garden,
which is very differ-
ent from a manicured garden. If something does die, you
don't mourn it—there's not a great big hole left because
there's so much richness, so much variety, so much more
life overall."

Sara Stein

If you've just purchased a new home—either newly built or just new to you—odds are that you have one of two landscapes to deal with: the land*scraped* lot the builder left for you or the inherited typical American landscape that came with the home.

What you will be converting to is either a totally or mostly native landscape that will be xeriscapic, and will more than likely be either conventionally styled (a la the Suhrens' home shown in Chapter 3) or a naturalistic landscape. If you're planning to design and install a natural landscape, skip over all the directions on how to save desirable non-natives.

In this chapter, we'll look at three scenarios that will help you deal with whatever landscape you are starting with. The steps presented for these scenarios should be executed in the order they are listed. In each, for example, you are advised to have a landscape plan, but *when* to think about the plan will vary depending on which scenario matches your circumstances.

This development in Virginia is starting out like most subdivisions; it is scraped clean of vegetation and leveled.

Scenario One: Converting from a Land*scraped* Lot

In many ways, if the lot is bare earth, you're in better shape than if you have an inherited traditional American landscape. Think of it as an empty canvas, with all possibilities open to you and little if anything that must first be undone. Of course, life being imperfect, there are probably a few problems associated with this "clean" start. For one thing, the builder may have scraped off all the topsoil, leaving you with subsoil, which can be like peeling back a banana skin and finding not a banana but another and even tougher peel. Or, he could have really done you a big "favor" and trucked in fresh topsoil, which nine times out of ten will be chock full of unpleasant surprises, such as nutgrass or crabgrass—things you'll spend the rest of your life fighting.

Many new homes, particularly those in subdivisions, are built on what used to be old farmland or pastures. There's virtually no vegetation to save; you're starting from scratch.

1. **Get a plan.** If you're not gifted at design or knowledgeable about plants, hire a landscape architect or landscape designer. You may balk at having to pay someone to design your landscape, but a good professional can suggest ideas that you might never have thought of and save you a lot of money in the long run. Many nurseries offer landscape design services. Some don't even charge, as long as you buy your plants from them. Of course, the landscape plan will probably be limited to their in-stock plants, and may not be what you want or need. If the nursery is a traditional one, you'll get precious few native options.

2. If your land is flat as a pancake, it doesn't have to stay that way. Aside from covering the plant materials themselves, and where they will go, a good plan will also look at the **topography**. Hire a bulldozer

Margaret and Richard Nakamura had a bare lot when they moved into their new home, and chose to go native in a more conventional style. The only lawn area is seen by the house and serves as a path to the backyard garden. Newly planted, these low-growing flowers will soon fill in and form a lush bed near the street. The landscape was designed by Sheryl McLaughlin at Native Sun Nursery in Austin, Texas.

(or have your designer hire one) to shape the land, both for drainage and aesthetic appeal. Your landscape will be much more attractive if you imitate nature's softly curving contours. The 'dozer driver can sculpt a pond or pool, a swale, or a berm. But be very specific about how and where you want the land shaped. And, if at all possible, have a responsible party overseeing the operation.

3. **Deal with the weeds.** If you plan on having a conventional lawn that you mow all the time, or a concrete patio, farm weeds (as opposed to lawn weeds) may not matter all that much. But if you plan to have a buffalograss lawn and a flagstone patio with tiny aromatic plants in the cracks, the weeds will matter a lot, just as they will wherever you plan for flower beds, meadows, shrubbery, or shade trees.

There are two eradication methods that seem to be successful. One is to plow up the roots and let an especially harsh winter or summer kill them. Of course, this requires cooperation from the weather. The other method is to let the soil settle and the weeds come up. Then spray them with glyphosate before they set seed. Do this three or four times until the weed seeds in the top inch (25 mm) of soil have been exhausted. As long as you don't disturb that top inch of soil, they shouldn't give you any more trouble; any weeds that appear in the future will come in via wind or birds. (I can hear you gasping in astonishment; are they really recommending a *herbicide*? In some cases, reluctantly, yes. Glyphosate is the least-toxic chemical you can use, and is found in several commercial brands, including Roundup. We've spoken to dozens of respected environmentalists who concede that this is, for the moment, the best recourse in eliminating noxious weeds from large areas, including restored prairies.) When you dig a hole to plant a tree, the disturbed soil is a magnet for weeds. Here, you don't want to use any chemicals that would harm the tree, so you'll have to weed around it for a season until the weeds are gone.

4. If you want to **enrich the soil** for a flower bed, instead of tilling in compost, spread an inch of compost on top. This method is called top-dressing.

5. It is best to **plant everywhere at once.** Bare soil is an invitation for weeds to blow in. Nature abhors a vacuum; nature believes that anything is better than nothing.

6. For **lawn areas,** sow seed or sod or do a combination of seed and plugs. Seed is cheaper and takes longer. Sod is expensive and instant. Sometimes, Sally recommends sodding around walks or at the bottom of slopes to prevent erosion, and seeding everywhere else. If you need to seed in late fall, and your lawn is a warm-season grass

like buffalograss that grows only when the soil is warm, sow a cool-season crop with it. There are many natives suitable for this. There are native cool-season grasses such as needle grasses, Junegrass, Indian ricegrass, or Canadian wild rye. There are annual spring wildflower mixes that contain lupines or California poppies. Sometimes the only thing you can find to buy is a non-native, annual rye. That's OK. It will eventually disappear. You just want to get the ground covered over the winter. If you want a meadow or prairie, just plant the full mix of seeds, and each species will germinate when conditions are right.

7. In **nonturf areas**, plant mostly nursery-grown plants rather than trying to start them from seed. Plant as many plants as you can find and afford, and top-dress the bare soil. If you want a richer soil, use compost. If you have high winds and you need a heavier mulch, use shredded bark. If your neighbors are setting bags of leaves or pine needles out on their curbs, rescue them from the landfill. If you live in the desert, spread two or three inches (5 or 8 cm) of decomposed granite.

8. Even highly drought-tolerant plants must be watered regularly to **get them established**. Trees and shrubs may need to be watered two or more years, depending on size. Water deeply and then let the soil dry out two or three inches (5 or 8 cm) to encourage deep root growth. Perennials usually need to be watered the first summer. Seed may need to be watered two or three times if there is no rain to get the seed to germinate. Much less watering is needed to get plants established in the North and the East than in the South and the Southwest. There are no real guidelines, as soil, rainfall, and shade or lack of it vary so much. It's like feeding a baby. Pay attention and use your own good judgment. Where it's very hot, dry,

or windy, use shade cloth or bits of old Christmas trees or some other kind of temporary shield to hold in the moisture.

Scenario Two: Converting from a Conventional Landscape

This is what most of you will be dealing with. The yard has been reasonably well-maintained, and the plants will be all or mostly non-xeriscapic exotics from the neighborhood nursery. The soil will more than likely be dead, the result of years of over-fertilization and compacting.

1. **Decide on a timetable.** Do you want to convert everything at once or do it in sections? If the latter, decide where to start. Doing it in sections has two big advantages: it's easier on your back and your wallet, and, if you have ultraconservative neighbors who might be shocked by your "radical" new landscape look, doing it in sections—one section every year or two—allows you to sneak up on them. Also, are you are going to convert the whole yard? Some people like to reserve a small area for a vegetable garden, or for flowers that are personal favorites but need more watering than the xeriscapic plants require.

2. **Quit watering** the future Xeriscape areas immediately. Watch what lives and what dies. Some plants may get stressed and start to host every bug and disease in town, but will take two or three years to die a painful death. Euthanasia is permitted. Some plants will be drought tolerant, but will have outgrown what they can support on rainfall alone. They may let some branches die and not others. You can either watch this process and let the plant choose the healthiest branches, or you can give the plant a severe pruning

When Sally and I moved into our Dallas home in 1979, we had inherited a conventional landscape with a St. Augustine lawn (dormant when this picture was taken in November) and a collection of non-native evergreens. The only natives we found on the property were some wood violets, which the previous owner apologized for. "I kept poisoning them, but they wouldn't go away," she told us. When we moved in 1996, I'm happy to report the violets were still there and doing fine.

Sally began the conversion process after seeing the water bills that first summer. For my part—being a sensitive, New Age guy—I hated seeing her out there pushing that lawn mower. She began with a ten-foot-by-ten-foot (3-m-by-3-m) patch at the lower right, by the street. It was an experimental process, using a variety of natives and non-natives. A year later, when she had a better idea what would work, she moved on to the next section. At the end of seven years, the lawn was completely gone and we had a naturalistic woodland garden. In this picture, some of the non-native evergreens are still there, but they would all be gone by year eight. To see how the front yard looked just before we moved, see Chapter 3.

Landscaping Revolutionary: Rochelle Whiteman

Natural landscapers sometimes incur the ire of neighbors who are uncomfortable with this style of gardening. Rochelle Whiteman had a refreshingly different experience—one that should encourage all those who want to get away from the drudgery of conventional landscaping.

In 1979, Rochelle and Paul Whiteman built a home in Glendale, Wisconsin, on the last undeveloped lot on their block. And while all the neighbors had, years earlier, put in conventional landscapes, Rochelle knew that this style was not for her. Trained as an artist, she found the lawn-centered look too sterile and uninteresting.

"At that time," she recalls, "I wasn't a plant person at all—I certainly didn't know Latin names!" So, she began with what she calls "typical plant choices, but massed for texture and used as ground cover. We planted anything that would spread easily. We had not yet learned that Wisconsin has native plants that are important to preserve."

She enlisted the help of her three children,

Maureen, Adam, and Lorelei, to "rescue" plastic bags of leaves discarded by neighbors, and spread the leaves about the quarter-acre (.1-ha) garden where they would break down and become nutrients. But these forays were usually conducted at night to spare her easily embarrassed children. They were also coached in how to answer classmates who wondered why their yard was "different," and not surprisingly, they grew up to become advocates for natural gardening.

As the years passed, her gardens matured and became something of a landmark in the community. Rochelle not only became more knowledgeable about native plants, she became the neighborhood expert on planting and propagating them. Rochelle found that her advice was sought by neighbors who not only

liked what they saw, but wanted to have natural landscapes of their own. To date, seven of her neighbors have converted to natural landscapes.

Charles and Anne Junkerman claim that Rochelle's garden was a major reason they moved into the community. "We were driving around and saw all these natural landscapes," says Charles, "and we thought that this looked like the kind of place we'd like to live." Rochelle encouraged them in their own landscaping plans, and gave them starter plants from her own garden. "Now," says Anne Junkerman, "we have a low-maintenance landscape that has a positive impact on the environment. We really like that."

"There's an ancient Hebrew story," says Rochelle, "that declares the planting of a tree to be a good deed of such a high order that even if the Messiah were to arrive at that moment, it would be incumbent on the individual to continue planting the tree. It is doubtful," she adds gleefully, "if this would hold true for a man mowing his lawn."

based on aesthetic considerations. **Keep the inherited lawn mowed and remove dead plants so that your devastation looks as neat and as deliberate as possible.**

3. **Watch the foundation of your house,** especially if your soil has a high clay content. You may have to water your foundation forever to keep your house in good shape. If this is the case, experiment with how little and how far out from the foundation you need to water and then install an irrigation system and a timer. If only the south and west sides of the house are affected, and there are no trees or shrubbery there, planting shade may be the best long-term solution.

4. **Be critical and coldhearted.** Once you know what is drought tolerant and what isn't, take a hard look at these plants from an aesthetic perspective and decide whether or not you like them, and whether you like where they are placed. It's OK to murder them or to find them alternate homes.

5. Based on your watering decisions and the plants you are keeping, now is the time to **make a plan.**

6. **Follow installation instructions** found above where they apply to you.

Scenario Three: Converting from a Heritage Landscape

You bought an old house in a historical neighborhood; maybe it was previously inhabited by an elderly person who didn't keep up with the maintenance. Maybe it was a rental property. It might even be a newly built home, but on an old and uncared-for residential lot. The point is, even though the plants may not look garden-magazine quality, they are drought tolerant and, with some attention, may be worth keeping.

1. **Assess what's already there.** If you can stand it, give yourself a year to watch

Nancy Powell bought an old farmhouse in Minnetonka, Minnesota, that was built about 1922. Around the foundation she found a lilac so old and big that it had engulfed the cement stepping stones that used to be a path beside it. Other shrubs were bridal wreath, a well-mannered bush honeysuckle, and a venerable antique rose that she liked so much she added two more. Where there was a lawn too steep to mow, she put in a native prairie. The whole landscape is drought tolerant and easy to care for. To Nancy's delight, the prairie attracted fireflies, butterflies, and dragonflies. One year a mallard nested in it. Flowers conspicuously in bloom are a rose, yarrow, black-eyed Susan, and northern bedstraw.

what comes up in different seasons. Take lots of pictures, and/or keep a garden journal to help your memory recall what they looked like at various times of the year. Often there are wonderful heritage bulbs you see only for a week or so in spring or fall. There may be irises or day lilies or peonies that look healthy but don't bloom. They may need to be dug up and divided. But there may be easier solutions. Maybe they aren't getting enough sunlight, so thin out the branches of that tree overhead. A good mulching with organically rich compost and minerals usually helps, because they have exhausted their spot of soil of the nutrients they especially need.

2. Scraggly shrubs sometimes turn out to be jewels. Let them flower and, if you like what you see, give the shrub some **judicious pruning**. Old shrubs often have thick twisting trunks and "artistic" shapes that just need a good pruning to be exquisitely beautiful. Occasionally, a shrub has been so badly pruned that you need to cut it to the ground and let it start over. These shrubs are often to be valued, for they have proven themselves well-adapted, and an old shrub will quickly regrow from a well-established root stock.

3. When weeding, **disturb the soil as little as possible**. Often antique garden treasures reappear once the greenbriar, buckthorn, poison ivy, or two million box elder saplings have been removed. With woody plants, cut them to ground level and immediately paint undiluted glyphosate directly on the moist fresh cut. This keeps them from resprouting.

4. **Base your landscape design on what you want to keep.** These plants are established and have proven themselves over a number of years. They will be the backbone of your new garden.

5. **Install** your new plants **and top-dress** with a mulch suitable for your area (see step 7 in Scenario One). If the soil is compacted and not even weeds are growing well, you have probably lost the microscopic organisms that make soil work. Scatter on compost starter before spreading on the mulch.

Follow these instructions and two things will happen: first you'll have an attractive landscape that delivers all the environmental and low-maintenance benefits we've been talking about, and second, you'll be showing your neighbors that going native isn't some wild-eyed, looney tunes concept, but a sensible and visually appealing idea that they may actually want to try themselves. Don't think that can happen? Then read about Rochelle Whiteman's experience.

Chapter 11

THIS TIME
THE LAND
WINS

"The sun, the moon,
   and the stars would have disappeared long ago, had
   they happened to be within the reach of predatory
   human hands."

Havelock Ellis

Each year, all across America, thousands of acres of uncultivated, natural land—woodlands, meadowlands, desert habitats, coastal scrub, and savannas—are transformed into homesites. The natural beauty of these places is a powerful draw for people wanting to escape the many woes of living in crowded urban and suburban areas. They want to get back to nature, breathe clean air, and hear birds singing outside their windows.

The irony is that by the time the moving vans pull up in front of these brand-new country homes, the beauty that first attracted these homeowners—the very character and personality of the land—has been destroyed.

The culprit is our traditional method of home construction. Bulldozers scrape the land clean of indigenous understory trees, shrubs, wildflowers, and grasses. Shade trees that were left standing very often die within the first few years anyway because of damage inflicted upon them during construction. I recall one classic example: when my wife was running her landscape design business in Dallas, she got a frantic call one day from a couple who had moved into a brand-new home just six months earlier. "Help," they cried, "our wonderful shade trees are dying. In fact, two are dead already!" The builder had not cut down the majestic and venerable trees, primarily because they added to the sales appeal of the house. But, being ignorant of how fragile trees can be, his work crews unwittingly committed several lethal acts that doomed them. In one case, several inches of dirt had been piled up around the flare at the base of the trunk, and that tree died of suffocation. Another tree had its bark girdled by construction equipment and was fated to succumb in a few more months. Still another tree suffered root damage when the workers washed out the cement mixer too close to it; the washout soaked down to the roots and poisoned them.

Another thing you can almost certainly count on is that the builder will truck in a couple of loads of topsoil after construction

The trees were all cut down and the land scraped clean to make room for this Virginia development. Notice the sapling in the foreground, a pathetic reminder of the verdant woodland that once occupied this site. With a little planning and creativity, these homes could have been surrounded by beautiful forests, and a valuable habitat could have been preserved.

is completed, bringing with it a host of unpleasant surprises: nutgrass, johnsongrass, and other noxious weeds that the new owners will have to live with for years. And, of course, the property will be relandscaped from scratch—at great cost—and usually with plants that have little or nothing to do with what had grown there originally.

The good news is that, today, all over the country, a handful of builders, landscape architects and designers, and, yes, homeowners themselves, are responding with a relatively new approach called "building inside nature's envelope"—a technique that preserves the integrity of the natural area. The Lady Bird Johnson Wildflower Center in Austin, Texas, was built using this technique. "During construction, if a conflict arose between the buildings and the land," says former executive director David Northington, "the land always won."

And, the homeowner gets one other enormous advantage by using this approach—

A protective fence surrounds the building site; outside the fence is the natural area, and it is sacrosanct!

personal plant favorites," says Davis, "including high-water-use tropicals or other exotics. These plants would be completely out of place in the natural habitat, but in the private zone they're fine."

The second area is the *transition zone* and can run from five to fifteen feet (150 to 460 cm) wide. It surrounds the residence, and all the work, equipment, and supplies are restricted to this zone during construction. Later, when the work is done, it will be revegetated. Both the private and transitional zones are considered to be inside the envelope.

The last area is the envelope itself—the undisturbed *natural zone*, and it consists of all the indigenous vegetation and topographical features, such as washes, rock formations, slopes, etc. It is *sacrosanct*!

To protect the natural zone, a fence is erected around the perimeter of the

very low maintenance. A preserved and mature natural landscape is the easiest, most foolproof kind of gardening imaginable.

How the Envelope Works

At Desert Highlands in Scottsdale, Arizona, the envelope is the standard for the entire development, and its mandatory use is written into the purchase agreement. But what if you are purchasing a plot out in the country where no rules and regulations have been established for preserving the natural land? By using the basic approach practiced by Gage Davis and the contractors working in this community, you can successfully introduce the envelope to your own property.

Your first step will be to divide your property into three areas. The first is the home itself, including driveway, patio, courtyard, and pool, and is designated the *private zone*. "This is where people can have their

By using the envelope technique, the finished home looks like it has been gently set down in the midst of the undisturbed natural setting. The mature and established landscape is preserved and a true sense of place is maintained.

transitional zone. And this is the key to the success of the building envelope: no workers, equipment, or building activity are permitted outside of that fence. The work crews aren't even allowed to eat their lunches out there. At Desert Highlands, sturdy chain-link fencing is used, but in other parts of the country where building techniques akin to the envelope are used, I've seen everything from snow fencing to simple rope or ribbon barriers employed. Clearly, the more formidable the fencing, the more assurance the property owner has that the envelope will be respected.

As soon as possible after you purchase the land, conduct a plant survey. Record all desirable plant materials on the site, both inside and outside the envelope, and mark them with various colored ribbons, denoting that they will be either transplanted or left alone. If you are unfamiliar with the local flora, you might hire a botanist from a local college or university, or a knowledgable person from a nursery. But be careful—just because someone is a professional plant person doesn't always mean they know anything about native plants. I've heard some real nutty opinions from so-called pros.

Bulldozers: Dozing at the Wheel

A few years back, our friend Ron lived through a landscaping nightmare. He'd purchased a lushly

Heavy construction equipment, such as bulldozers, can do tremendous damage to the natural vegetation on a property. Trees that aren't mowed down outright can also be girdled, eventually killing them.

wooded lot on the outskirts of Dallas and planned to build his home there. Ron is an architect, and he knows how to preserve trees. Still, he couldn't have foreseen what eventually happened.

The trouble began because another home was being built on the adjoining lot. One day, our friend discovered that the neighbor's bulldozer had run amock on Ron's property and had destroyed a number of mature trees. Of course, Ron eventually collected damages, but let's face it, no amount of money can replace a thirty-year-old tree. Not in less than thirty years, that is.

But the horror story didn't end there. When it came time for Ron to build his own house, he gave specific instructions to his own bulldozer operator. He marked the trees that were to be saved with orange ribbons, and even took time off from work to stand around and supervise. Trouble was, the operator got back from lunch before Ron, and in less than fifteen minutes six more perfectly healthy, mature trees had been leveled. To paraphrase writer P. J. O'Rourke, giving a bulldozer to some guys is like giving liquor and car keys to teenaged boys.

The envelope is not just for new homes way out in the boondocks. This home was built by Cindy Hollar and Kevin Tennison on a modestly sized suburban lot in Arlington, Texas, that had been left undeveloped. The lot was surrounded by conventionally landscaped homes; now the couple's home is surrounded by woods, giving them privacy and an effective sound buffer. They report lower air-conditioning bills, as well.

Once you have a good plant survey, you'll be able to determine what you want to save and what is expendable. A tree, for instance, that looks great at first glance may be too old or diseased to warrant the trouble of transplanting. Plants within the envelope that are to be saved should then be carefully dug up, boxed, and taken out of harm's way. Put them on a drip irrigation system to await replanting during the revegetation phase after construction.

Smaller vegetation, such as ground covers, would be impractical to dig up and keep alive during the construction period. In such cases, collect cuttings and seeds, and then contract with a local nursery to grow them for you so they'll be ready for transplanting as soon as the builders pack up and leave. And while you're having that plant survey done, make sure specific market values are placed on all your major plants—the ones that, if destroyed, would affect the financial as well as aesthetic value of your property. Trees that are too large to be replaced should have "penalty" prices put on them. When the Lady Bird Johnson Wildflower Center was built, trees were hung with large price tags displaying large prices ranging from $2,500 to $23,000!

At Desert Highlands, even the soil within both the private and transitional areas is scraped up and set aside, like the plants, to be spread out around the home after construction. Remember—that soil is full of nutrients and seeds that are natural to the site, and important to its future vitality. Do *not* bring in outside topsoils!

You will also work closely with your architect or designer to incorporate as much of the natural lay of the land as practical. You aren't just preserving vegetation, you're preserving the integrity and character of the land.

One last recommendation: from the outset, there must be a clear understanding that your contractor is responsible for the vegetation in the natural area and it must be protected. If possible, have the contractor present on-site when the plant survey is conducted. It's a good way to emphasize the importance you place on the plants' preservation. If you think a sincere promise and a firm handshake from the contractor will guarantee that your natural area will be protected, think again! *Put everything in writing.* Your contractor should agree to pay the full fair market value of any plants his or her people kill or injure. And that does *not* mean replacing a thirty-year-old shade tree with a five-gallon sapling. If he or she balks, get another contractor.

Suburban Envelopes

In case you're thinking that the envelope applies only to large-scale developments way out in the boonies, let's look at a few excellent envelope homes in suburbia—on lots that developers or builders hadn't gotten to yet. Often, these lots are sandwiched in between conventionally landscaped homes. We found one such envelope home in Arlington, Texas. It belonged to Cindy Hollar and Kevin Tennison. When they found the one-third-acre (.13-ha) lot, it was chock-full of trees and understory, and the couple was reluctant to disturb its natural beauty.

The couple interviewed four architects before finding one who understood what they were after and was simpatico with the concept. When we visited the completed home, one of the neighbors came outside and told us, wistfully, that she'd have loved having a similar landscape—had she only known it was possible.

The woodland home that Mary and Dick Stanley built in Dellwood, Minnesota, demonstrated for us how to incorporate specific features of the property into the overall design. Several trees that might have been cut down to make room for a deck or walkway were retained, and the construction virtually embraced these trees. A fish pond occupied a corner of their lot, but was so close to where they would be building that it might have been filled in and lost had the Stanleys not worked closely with a cooperative builder to save it.

And in case you're wondering, yes, the envelope concept also works well in nonresidential construction. We saw one fine example outside Milwaukee, Wisconsin. The corporate home of Marquette Electronics is nestled in a lush woodland setting, much of which would have been lost had conventional construction methods been employed.

Envelope Communities

It's not just individual homeowners and developers who are turning to this method of building in natural areas. Municipalities, too, are adopting the envelope approach. In Colorado, Tom Newland, former deputy director for Pitkin County Public Works, says that preserving the natural beauty in and around Aspen is so important that the building envelope has become a part of the county's building codes. "This is a major resort," says Newland, "and our natural, rural scenery is a vital part of the Aspen experience. You just can't build here without using the envelope."

The Woodlands, a twenty-year-old, twenty-five-thousand-acre (10,125-ha) incorporated residential community forty miles (64 km) north of Houston, was an early advocate of the envelope technique. The aim, as stated in the residents' guide, was and is "to live in harmony with nature." Homes are tucked back among the pines and live oaks, and even commercial areas—shops, gas stations, and fast-food outlets—are discreetly screened by canopy and understory trees.

A home in The Woodlands as it was originally meant to be. Today, as the influence of the landscaping revolution is being felt more and more, many of the landscapes that had once been converted to more conventional styles are now reconverting back to the natural look.

Unfortunately, the envelope philosophy was never made a part of the residents' covenants, so many of the homeowners strayed from the initial concept. "The people like being surrounded by the forest," observes Wanda Jones, a landscape designer who lives and works in The Woodlands, "but over the years, many have brought in their own landscapers, who cut down most of the trees right around their homes and put in clipped hedges, exotic plants, and lawns—a more conventional look." Today, with natural landscaping growing in popularity, Wanda's company, Nature's Touch, is busy restoring many of those conventional landscapes back into natural ones.

Practicing What We Preach

Our own quest for a personal Eden came to an end on Thanksgiving 1994, when we went to Taos, New Mexico, to celebrate with friends. On a mountainside thirty minutes north of the picturesque art colony and ski mecca we found three acres (1.2 ha) of piñons, junipers, and ponderosa pines . . . and a picture-postcard view of Taos Mountain. Sally and I looked at each other, grinned like idiots, and decided to grab it. A year later we began to build.

For most people, selecting the right architect is a major decision. While Cindy Hollar and Kevin Tennison had to interview four architects, our task was much easier. We already knew who we wanted. I had known our architect, Stephen Merdler of Santa Fe, since we were kids growing up in New Jersey; his mother had actually played matchmaker for my parents in prewar Poland. Sally and I had long admired his fluid and spacious adobe designs, and as soon as we bought the land in Taos, we knew we'd be giving Stephen a call.

While Stephen had never actually designed a home with the envelope, he was immediately in synch with our desires, and produced a knockout plan for our home that fit comfortably onto our sloping land. He avoided the prime trees and situated the well, propane tank, and septic system where they would be least disruptive. Installing these features frequently causes a great deal of unnecessary destruction to the property.

An equally important decision is picking the contractor. Contractors must not only do the kind of quality work you demand, they must do it in conjunction with the envelope—

Landscaping Revolutionary: Gage Davis

Nowhere is the envelope better demonstrated than in Scottsdale, Arizona, thanks in large measure to Gage Davis. In 1981, Davis—a triple-threat individual who is an architect, landscape architect, and urban planner—combined his skills and introduced the envelope approach at Desert Highlands, an 850-acre (344-ha) residential community in North Scottsdale.

"The desert is a terribly fragile environment," says Davis, "easy to destroy and very slow to recover. It's possible to go out into the desert and see clear signs of Indian encampments a hundred or more years old."

Because of that, Desert Highlands offered a particularly good environment to prove the effectiveness of the envelope. Situated at the base of picturesque Pinnacle Peak, the land is a prime example of the ruggedly beautiful Sonoran Desert.

The topography consists of ravines, washes, dramatic rock outcroppings, and fields of boulders. It is also alive with a wide variety of wildlife: desert tortoises, colorful chuckwalla lizards, roadrunners, and hummingbirds galore, as well as a vast palette of indigenous flora, from armies of

stately saguaros and luminescent backlit chollas, to the softer, gentler paloverdes, creosotes, fairydusters, penstemons, and verbenas.

Davis's goal was a subtle blending of people, structures, and desert habitat into a harmonious and aesthetically pleasing community.

a technique with which they will probably be unfamilar. Besides, even the best-intentioned builder will be bound by years of doing it the old way. Your average builder just isn't happy unless he or she can clear a swath around the building site as wide as a football field. Needless to say, establishing the fence line provoked an especially passionate debate. "I just can't work in such a confined area," our builder, Wade Elston, complained. "It's not realistic."

"That tree will *not* be cut down," we countered.

The trick is to be firm but reasonable. You need the builder's goodwill and cooperation if the work of the architect is not to be undone. We all made concessions; we agreed that one tree we especially loved really had to go, while Wade found out that, yes, by golly, he could work in less space. In the end, he admitted that the job had been a valuable learning experience for him, and he looked forward to taking on more envelope projects.

Nothing beats firsthand experience for separating theory from reality. For one thing, we learned that trees that sit directly on the homesite don't always have to be cut down. Thanks to Wade's negotiations with a local nursery, twenty-two piñons were dug up and transported to the nursery to be sold. Three others were replanted elsewhere on our property. Cost to us? Nada!

We also learned that you can save a tree and then lose it long after construction is over. Three piñons that abutted our patio began to look stressed a full year and a half after we'd moved in. We consulted a local arborist and learned that three factors had combined to endanger the trees. For one thing, we'd just come through an abnormally dry winter. Also, the downhill position of the house now impeded the snow runoff the trees would ordinarily have enjoyed. Lastly, of course, the construction—no matter how carefully done—did injure some of the roots and made the trees vulnerable.

We began watering the trees immediately and as of this writing, we saved all of them. However, one will probably die.

Using the envelope takes some foresight and planning. But in the end, when you are sitting out on your patio, enjoying the performances of the songbirds and the aerobatics of the butterflies and listening to the breeze stirring the branches of those trees you saved—you'll agree that preserving your natural habitat was one of the smartest things you ever did.

Our home outside Taos is snugly nestled into the piñons and junipers, thanks to the envelope technique.

Self-sustaining envelope communities are springing up all over the country. This one is on Dewees Island, South Carolina. You arrive at this beautiful 1,206-acre barrier island by ferry, a fifteen-minute ride. When you get there, transportation is provided by a fleet of battery-powered golf carts. And, according to the development's subdivision policy, "Formal lawns are not allowed. Landscape plants must be native to the coastal plain barrier island."

Chapter 12

WEEDING OUT BAD WEED LAWS

"I have a child, and I feel it's important that I show him that we can exist within nature's way."

**Sandra Bell
Statement to a Toronto
Court as She Defended Her
Right to Have a Natural
Landscape**

Picture this: Your mailman arrives and drops off the usual batch of bills, supermarket flyers, and mail-order catalogs. But what's this? Something from the city! It looks important—even ominous. You read the official epistle—and you are so stunned you have to sit down. It reads:

> *Your neighbors have lodged a complaint against your home. It has been determined that your home is painted in a color that does not conform to neighborhood standards. You have ten days from receipt of this notice to repaint your home with one of the three shades of white deemed acceptable by your neighbors. If this is not done, the city will paint it for you, at your expense.*

If this sounds like something out of Orwell or Kafka, consider that every year, all over the country, hundreds of homeowners receive similar notices from their city governments. The difference is that these complaints are not about the color these people selected for their homes, but the plants they selected for their landscapes! Accused of growing "weeds," these homeowners are often prosecuted by their municipalities and persecuted by their neighbors.

We're not making this up. It happened to Evelyn Connors in Tulsa, Oklahoma.

It happened to Nancy and Walter Stewart in Potomac, Maryland.

It happened to Sandra Bell in Toronto, Canada.

It happened to Ned Fritz in Dallas, Texas.

It happened to Stephen Kenney in New York State.

It happened to Marie Wojciechowski in Chicago.

It happened to Midge Erskine in Midland, Texas.

And, should you deviate from the traditional manicured lawn and box hedge landscape, choosing instead to use native plants in a more natural landscape, it could happen to you!

What Is a Weed, Anyway?

Most people would say that a weed is a plant that doesn't belong and is unwanted. If you accept this definition, then logically you cannot call any native plant a weed. After all, what is more appropriate to a site than a plant that is indigenous to it? True weeds are alien invaders that arrived on these shores in a variety of ways—in shipments of fruits and vegetables, in the dirt that old-time sailing ships used as ballast, on the soles of travelers' boots, or in animal droppings. They became naturalized and thrived, usually in disturbed areas such as vacant lots, utility cuts through woodlands, and cultivated farmlands. Weeds are the result of civilization and cultivation. As author Michael Pollan points out, you just don't find weeds in nature.

In the early part of this century, the first weed laws were enacted for the benefit of farmers. These laws were intended to regulate specific plants—so-called noxious weeds—that were harmful to agriculture. These weeds included crabgrass, chickweed, johnsongrass, bindweed, and a variety of thistles. These laws were necessary and beneficial, and were usually enacted at the state level.

Years later, someone noticed that many of the weeds that plagued farmers were showing up in residential neighborhoods. So counties, municipalities, and eventually even subdivisions began enacting their own weed laws and covenants. More often than not, these were strictures that outlawed not specific noxious species, but herbaceous vegetation that had grown up higher than the arbitrary height restrictions imposed by the community.

Before I go further, I should state that, used properly, community weed laws are not necessarily bad—they protect our property values from neighbors who allow their yards to run amok and become trashy. No one wants this. The problem arises when, too often, the powers-that-be just can't tell the difference between noxious weeds and healthy natural vegetation. Plants get labeled as weeds simply because they aren't standard and familiar nursery stock.

These same laws are also used against homeowners who deviate from the conventional manicured look by opting for natural or naturalistic landscapes that attract wildlife, require less irrigation and toxic chemicals, and reflect the uniqueness of their part of the country.

The Land Ethic

Wildflowers have long had a place in American gardening, although they were not taken seriously by "civilized" gardeners who eschewed native flora in favor of imported exotics. In the 1930s, the voice of naturalist/philosopher Aldo Leopold was raised. In Leopold's view, "a thing is right when it tends to preserve the stability and integrity of a biotic community; it is wrong when it tends otherwise." The land ethic he espoused offered a springboard for what has become the science of restoration ecology and the practice of natural landscaping.

Leopold believed that this land ethic would never succeed unless it was practiced by private citizens. But it wasn't until the 1970s that the natural landscaping movement really got going. A growing number of people began to realize that we as a society probably hadn't been the good stewards our Judeo-Christian heritage enjoins us to be. Like an alarm clock at 3 A.M., Rachel Carson's *Silent Spring* aroused us to environmental dangers that we had, until then, either ignored or been ignorant of. Soon a growing list of books and articles and environmental advocates gave us a new awareness of our planet and a new vocabulary: ecosystem, greenhouse effect, acid rain, biodiversity, chloroflourocarbons, and deforestation.

But disappearing rain forests, polluted oceans, and endangered ozone layers are big and highly technical issues, leaving the average concerned citizen feeling overwhelmed and impotent. The one area where they felt they could make a positive difference was in how they landscaped around their homes. And so they adopted more natural landscapes, using native and well-naturalized flora, and allowed them to grow the way Mother Nature had intended.

Needless to say, their "deviant" behavior did not go unnoticed, and soon they were under attack from neighbors and local officials who found this "undisciplined" style unsettling. British philosopher John Stuart Mill hit the nail on the head when he observed that every great movement is initially greeted with ridicule . . . and worse.

Weed laws are not of themselves bad; used correctly they protect us from run-amok yards and messy neighbors that can affect our own property values. The trouble arises when these laws are used against environmentally responsible homeowners who choose a more naturalistic landscape.

Heroes of the Landscaping Revolution

In 1986, Nancy and Walter Stewart, of Potomac, Maryland, stopped mowing their seven-acre (2.8-ha) yard and allowed it to become a natural meadow. It was soon lush with wildflowers and native meadow grasses. The meadow thrived on rainfall alone, got mowed just twice a year, and got zero pesticides. But the neighbors saw only weeds, and were furious. One sent the Stewarts an anonymous letter calling their meadow a "disgrace."

When the county cited the couple, Nancy, a Justice Department attorney, threatened a legal challenge, and the county backed down. It also amended the law to permit meadow gardens as long as a mowed strip surrounded it.

Ned Fritz, a Dallas attorney and author (*Clearcutting: A Crime Against Nature*), had to go to court when he was cited for growing sunflowers, goldenrod, and Virginia wild rye in his front yard. City prosecutors claimed Fritz was creating a health hazard by permitting "weeds" to grow above twelve inches (30 cm). Expert defense witnesses countered that the plants were not weeds because they did not meet the accepted definition of "unwanted plants." The jury ruled in favor of Fritz and his "weeds."

Canadian Sandra Bell also went to court to establish her right to a natural landscape. Bell testified that when she had moved into her Toronto home in 1990, the front yard contained only three species: Virginia creeper, sedum, and a Kentucky bluegrass lawn. Sandra's aim was to create an "environmentally sound" natural landscape containing over forty different species—an excellent example of biodiversity.

At Sandra's trial, York University Professor Harry Merren testified that traditional landscapes "express an urge to dominate or control nature," while natural gardens are "a commitment to living in greater harmony with nature." The Canadian appeals court found that the practice of natural landscaping was a matter of conscience that could not be prohibited without a compelling reason. Sandra joined a growing roster of natural landscapers who had beaten City Hall.

For other natural landscapers, the path to victory is sometimes more difficult. One of the few to lose a case was New York State resident Stephen Kenney. The housing development where he resided brought legal action against him because he had planted a meadow of black-eyed Susans, coneflowers, and familiar naturalized exotics such as bachelor's buttons and ox-eye daisies. Refusing to cut his meadow down, Kenney was fined $50 a day until he "saw the light" and conformed. He ran up a total fine of $30,000, but an appeals court reduced the amount to $500. Still, neighbors continued to complain, threatening him by vandalizing the meadow and shooting birds that were attracted to this habitat. Eventually, Kenney was forced out of his home. He now lives in another state.

The case of the "Chicago Five" is ironic because three of the defendants were practicing their natural gardening *in cooperation with a branch of the local government*. Mike Regenfuss was cultivating a natural landscape as part of a restoration project sponsored by Cook County and the Nature Conservancy; Debra Petro was growing native Illinois prairie and savanna plants as part of a city prairie-reconstruction project; and Rich Hyerczyk was growing native plants in his role as regional ecologist for a county restoration program.

Moreover, these government agencies were going more natural not just for aesthetic and environmental reasons, but also because the municipal prairie landscapes were deemed to be economical. By allowing prairie grasses and wildflowers to grow along roadsides, for example, the state's Department of

Transportation reduced gas consumption, wear and tear on equipment, and labor costs involved in mowing.

Ultimately, Regenfuss, Petro, and Hyerczyk—plus two other natural landscapers—grew tired of being threatened with prosecution for their labors and filed suit in 1991 to have the Chicago Weed Ordinance declared unconstitutional. They stated that the very government that was threatening to bring suit against them was itself attempting to expand its own natural plantings. In the end, the city assured the court that legitimate natural landscapers had nothing to fear from them, and in the years since no further action was taken against these five individuals or any other Chicagoans—but the weed law remains on the books.

The Trend Toward Tolerance

The most common and onerous weed laws are called fiat laws and were first enacted in the 1940s. A good example is Chicago's ordinance, which flatly outlaws "any weeds in excess of an average height of ten inches."

Landscape Revolutionary: Evelyn Connors

Do these look like weeds to you? One of Evelyn Connors's neighbors thought they did, and got the city of Tulsa to cite the eighty-two-year-old widow.

One sunny June afternoon in 1995, after conducting a tour of her garden for several hundred visitors, Evelyn received a notice from her city government ordering her to mow down her "weeds," which were in fact a mass of beautiful native purple coneflowers. An anonymous neighbor (it's interesting how often these people are anonymous) didn't like them and made an official complaint. Tulsa soon learned that it had picked on the wrong eighty-two-year-old widow.

Evelyn, an avid gardener, contacted the *Tulsa World*, and the next day she was front-page news. Not just in Tulsa, but all over the country. Local disk jockeys contributed to her growing fame by asking listeners to drive by her home; if they approved of her landscape, they were to honk their horns. The din was terrific! Before long, Evelyn was receiving letters of support from sympathetic homeowners and children from California to the Carolinas. Many arrived in her mailbox with no better address than "The Wildflower Lady, Tulsa, Oklahoma." There was even talk of a TV movie about her. Before long the mayor came to her home, oohed and aahed over her naturalistic garden, apologized for all the fuss, and rescinded the citation.

There is no attempt to define what a weed is, although it is commonly understood to be any plant that is not familiar nursery stock and exceeds the arbitrary height.

Homeowners who cultivate meadows, woodlands, and other natural and healthy habitats around their homes are often just as likely to get cited by these fiat laws as homeowners who allow their front yards to become overgrown with crabgrass, chickweed, smooth brome, bindweed, and other noxious vegetation.

A second, more tolerant weed law, allows natural landscaping—but only if the homeowner obtains municipal permission first. Madison, Wisconsin, was the first major city to recognize the legitimacy of natural landscapes by enacting an ordinance that requires the homeowner to file an application and then get a majority of the neighbors to approve. While better than the fiat laws, this ordinance still places unnecessary restrictions on the property owner's right to landscape naturally.

The ordinances enacted in White Bear Lake, Minnesota, and Lawrence, Kansas, to name just two, represent the third-generation weed law. While natural landscaping is permitted without neighbor approval or city permission, there are two provisos: (1) true weeds and other rank vegetation are prohibited, and (2) there must be a setback along the front and/or perimeters of the lot where vegetation may not exceed a certain height, such as ten or twelve inches (25 or 30 cm). This height restriction does not include trees and shrubs. A similar statewide law is being considered by the Nebraska legislature.

Long Grove, Illinois, is one of a growing number of communities that recognize the environmental benefits of having naturalistic landscaping and encourage residents to surround their home with "prairie" landscapes that include both native and well-adapted, noninvasive naturalized plants.

The fourth generation of weed laws is in fact not a weed law at all, but official sanction of natural landscapes. Communities such as Long Grove, Illinois, and Fort Collins, Colorado, have no laws restricting plant height, and actually encourage the use of native plants and natural landscapes. These communities recognize that humans and nature are interconnected and interdependent.

Myths and Misconceptions

Fiat weed laws are being challenged more and more, with a growing rate of success. The Wild Ones, for example, is in the vanguard of the effort to change outdated weed laws by emphasizing cooperation and education. Sometimes victory is achieved on constitutional grounds, more often by exposing the misconceptions people have about natural landscapes. When misconceptions give way to knowledge, then fiat laws also give way— first to tolerance, then acceptance, and finally encouragement.

Misconception: Natural Landscapes Harbor Vermin

Fact: Vermin live in garbage. Natural landscapes have nothing in them to attract or sustain vermin. Native rodents—commonly called field mice—are grain eaters and are not classified as vermin. Generally, homeowners have far less to fear from them than from urbanized pests (Norway rats and roaches), which carry and spread disease.

Interestingly, the only time I ever saw a rat in a residential neighborhood, it was crossing the street in a suburb of Austin, Texas, where all the homes had well-manicured traditional landscapes.

Another issue is Lyme disease, a serious consideration in many parts of the country. Exposure to the *Ixodes* tick, which spreads the disease, can occur in both natural and conventional landscapes, since white-tailed deer, white-footed mice, birds, raccoons, and even dogs and cats can be transporters of the ticks. Dr. Ken Pinkston at Oklahoma State University's entomology department states that he is "unaware of any studies that show an increase in tick-borne diseases in areas with natural landscapes." Exposure can be minimized in a natural landscape by incorporating low mowed areas, gravel or wood-chip paths, and by staying out of higher vegetation.

Misconception: Natural Landscapes Are Fire Hazards

Fact: The fire hazard in any landscape— natural or conventional—comes from dead wood and other dry vegetation. Well-cared for natural landscapes are composed mostly of green, leafy materials that just don't burn. While prairie grasses are flammable, they burn out too quickly to pose a threat to a house.

Misconception: Natural Landscapes Harbor Mosquitoes

Fact: Mosquito larvae are bred in standing water, not native vegetation. Natural landscapes with ponds also tend to have fish that devour larvae. These landscapes also attract birds and predator insects that feast on any mosquitoes that make it to adulthood.

Misconception: Natural Landscapes Produce Allergy-Causing Pollen

Fact: A major cause of watery eyes and sniffles is airborne pollen from ragweed, which is found in disturbed areas such as vacant lots, not in healthy natural landscapes. Showy flowers also have pollen, but this is carried about by insects and hummingbirds; it never gets into the air to become an irritant. Some botanists actually contend that the exotic plants found in conventional landscapes cause more allergenic pollen than do natives.

You may have noticed that the matter of aesthetics hasn't been mentioned. That's because, in the final analysis, the aesthetics argument is illogical. Some homeowners think pink flamingos, plastic sunflowers, concrete deer, and Astroturfed front stoops are attractive, and it's their right to have them. Why then shouldn't homeowners also be granted the right to have environmentally friendly natural landscapes that are both attractive and beneficial?

Until that day comes, natural landscapers may have to face off with neighbors and city officials who dislike and disagree with the way they choose to garden. It would be nice if all judges shared the sentiments of Canadian Justice Fairgrieve, who wrote, "The objective of creating neat, conventionally pleasant residential yards does not warrant a complete denial of the right to express a differing view of man's relationship with nature."

Landscaping Revolutionary: Bret Rappaport

"Where is it written," asks Chicago attorney Bret Rappaport, "that everyone must have the same kind of landscape?" He then answers his own question. "If you read any of the countless municipal weed ordinances from around the country, you get the impression that this is exactly what is intended. Everyone must conform to some 'ideal' image of a home landscape, that is, the conventional manicured lawn—crisply pruned boxhedge—row of annuals look."

When he graduated from law school and went to work at a prestigious Chicago law firm, Bret had no idea that he would one day become a champion for homeowners' rights to have more environmentally friendly landscapes. But in 1991, while serving as a volunteer with the Sierra Club Lawyers Roundtable, he was asked by five Chicago homeowners to represent them in a suit against that city. Feeling that the city's weed ordinance was unconstitutional, arbitrary, and decidedly antienvironment, they hoped to overturn it.

A number of questions immediately arose in Bret's legalistic mind. For instance, what exactly is meant by "weeds"? In fact, as Bret was to learn, weeds do not occur in nature. They are alien invaders—such as johnsongrass and nutgrass—that thrive in disturbed areas. Often they arrive in home landscapes with a truckload of topsoil.

Bret also wondered how one calculates an "average" height. Does the city go around measuring every single plant in a yard? Since plants grow, at what point in the

Nobody is attacking these people for their choice of yard art. Yet homeowners who choose to have environmentally responsible landscapes are prosecuted by municipalities and persecuted by neighbors all the time. The good news is, the tide is turning. Unfair weed laws are being overturned, and more and more people are coming to recognize the benefits of natural landscapes.

growth process is the measurement taken? Or does someone take the average height of a plant species and then compare it to the average heights of all the other species? Clearly, Bret saw, this was a can of worms!

Because this was his first exposure to weed ordinances, Bret began by looking for legal precedents. He was amazed to discover that while virtually all communities have weed laws, very few had ever been challenged in court. "Weed ordinances are usually treated like traffic tickets," he says. "People just don't bother to fight them."

Largely because of his involvement in this case, which generated national interest (cnn and cbs appeared on the scene to report the results, and the story went out over the wire services), Bret has become a big advocate of natural landscaping and served as president of the Wild Ones, an eleven-state organization dedicated to promoting natural landscaping. "We grant our neighbors the right to have shaved lawns or colored gravel, tacky concrete statuary, and Astroturf on the front porch," says Bret. "It's only fair that we also grant homeowners the right to have natural landscapes, which are far more beneficial."

Want more information about combating unfair weed ordinances? Write to The John Marshall Law School for a copy of Bret Rappaport's article in the summer 1993 issue of *The John Marshall Law Review*, volume 26, number 4. The address is 315 South Plymouth Court, Chicago, Illinois 60604. Include a check or money order for $5 plus postage. For a free copy of *Source Book on Natural Landscaping for Local Officials*, write to: Northern Illinois Planning Commission, 222 South Riverside Plaza, Chicago, Illinois 60606. Or visit the epa's web site at www.epe.gov/green acres.

Make Your Natural Landscape Acceptable

1. Add human touches to your natural landscape: a bench, a stone pathway, a birdbath. This makes your landscape look more "planned" and designed. This simple step pacifies many otherwise hostile neighbors.

2. Put up a small sign designating your property as a wildlife sanctuary or natural zone. In Texas, natural landscapers can earn a "Texas Wildscapes" sign by meeting the requirements of the state's Parks and Wildlife Department.

3. Invite the neighbors over and introduce them to your garden. Explain why it's the way it is, and how it benefits everyone.

4. Frame your landscape with a mowed area of grass or ground covers, or a low stone wall. This creates a tended and intended look. Suppose you threw paint on your wall. You'd have a mess. But put a picture frame around the splotch and suddenly it can be accepted—if not actually appreciated—as art.

5. Work with community officials to rewrite oppressive weed laws. Establish a list of noxious weeds that ought to be outlawed, while protecting beneficial plants. Interestingly, many municipalities allow natural areas in parks and highway medians, but not around residences. This inconsistency works to your advantage.

Ultimately, community acceptance will come about only with education and exposure to natural landscapes.

Chapter 13

WHO'S AFRAID OF VIRGINIA CREEPER?

"We will conserve only what we love,
we will love only what we understand,
and we will understand only what we are taught."

Baba Dioum
African Conservationist

Why is the conventional landscape still so much a part of our lives? Back in Chapter 1, we looked at some of the possibilities: from the "it's in the genes" theory to our all-too-human reluctance to be different—the "tyranny of the neighbors" syndrome. But do you know what I think the basic bottom-line reason is? It's simple. We're out of touch with the natural world and how it works. Educator Lewis Thomas once wrote, "The only solid piece of scientific truth about which I feel totally confident is that we are profoundly ignorant about nature."

For example, the folks at the National Zoo in Washington, D.C., conducted a poll a few years back to find out what people knew about pollination. The answer was, not much. Over 75 percent of their visitors didn't know the purpose of pollination. Most of them knew that pollen could make you sneeze, but that about exhausted their knowledge on the subject.

So what? you ask? So this: According to Harvard's Edward O. Wilson, "Eighty percent of the species of our food plants . . . depend on polination." No pollination, no fruits, no veggies, no grains. Yet there is overwhelming evidence that pollinators are declining all over the world. And conventional gardening, which includes the liberal use of pesticides, contributes to this decline. If we were more aware of just how vital pollination is to our lives, would we be less inclined to reach for the bug spray?

Another example: We grew up with the notion that plants have to be watered. But do you recall anyone telling you that plants can be overwatered? Incredibly, that bit of information seems never to have reached the company that was hired to install and maintain the landscape on the grounds of a corporate headquarters in north Texas. The job started out with all the right intentions, and everyone concerned went to great pains to preserve the existing natural landscape, which included a profusion of native wildflowers. But, because the decision makers were ignorant about how these plants grew, they made two fatal mistakes. First, they installed a sprinkler system. Their second mistake? They used it. The wildflowers drowned and have never come back.

Ignorance about our natural world has consequences—some are far-reaching, some are humorous, and some make you wonder if you should laugh or cry. I think of a couple who had spent several years designing and cultivating a beautiful native landscape around their home. Their pride and joy was the spectacular masses of Virginia creeper

National Zoo in Washington, D.C.

that clambered over the fence surrounding their yard. In the fall, this vine turns a startlingly vibrant red, especially when backlit. Unfortunately, the couple had to move and sold their home—and landscape—to people who knew next to nothing about gardening. They took one look at the Virginia creeper and had it pulled out—fast! They had mistaken it for poison ivy.

The thing about ignorance is that it breeds misunderstandings, discomfort, even fear. My own Aunt Inka, who lives in New York, is a very bright lady and could hold her own in a conversation about opera with Pavarotti. So why won't she come to visit us at our home in the mountains of northern New Mexico? Because, in her own words, "When I see two bushes together, I get nervous!" A city dweller from the time she was a child in Poland, she also informed me that she'd feel safer walking in Times Square at midnight than in the woods at noon.

My aunt is not unique. When comedian Woody Allen was filming *A Midsummer's Night Sex Comedy*, one scene called for him to fall into a country lake. He couldn't bring himself to do it. "There are *live things* in there," he explained, no doubt seeing himself awash in slimy eels and razor-toothed piranhas. A double was recruited to go into the drink for him. Later, when it came time to shoot the close-up, Allen held firm and refused even to have lake water poured over him. Instead, he was doused with bottles of Evian.

A bit extreme? Maybe. But then explain the outcry when an elementary school in Wisconsin proposed installing a natural garden around the building. The parents strongly objected because they were afraid that *rabbits would jump out and scare the children*!

And if you think that kids are more savvy about nature than their parents, think again. During a field trip through a demonstration vegetable garden in Dallas, at least half of the fourth-graders expressed amazement when they saw that carrots grew in the ground. And when a southern university tested youngsters to see how well they could identify various botanical smells, most of the kids identified lemon peel as dishwashing detergent.

What's up, Doc? This kid's eyebrows when he learned that carrots actually grow in the ground! A startling revelation to a lot of fourth-graders on a Texas field trip.

Is this how your kids learn about nature? As terrific as many of these programs are, they are no substitute for getting out there in a forest or meadow and experiencing the natural world firsthand.

Nature via the VCR

While many children may not be afraid of nature, most are indifferent to it—which is just as dangerous. So far as they can see, nature doesn't impact directly on their lives. It simply isn't relevant. This is especially true of young people growing up in urban and suburban neighborhoods.

Of course, there are many others—children and adults—who are neither fearful nor indifferent to nature. These folks think that nature is swell—as long as it's kept at arm's length. In his book, *The Value of Life*, Stephen Kellert points out that "For the majority of Americans, the vicarious experience of . . . zoos, film, television, and other indirect means, remains the predominant basis for encountering nature and living diversity."

Craig Johnson, director of education at the Morton Arboretum in Chicago, agrees, saying, "At Morton, all our environmental programs require the participants to be outdoors—to make firsthand discoveries. In the act of discovery, a bond is made with nature."

Sadly, this attitude is all too rare, and you have to wonder about the fate of our planet when our youngsters view a meadow or a patch of woods as unfamiliar territory, as mysterious as the dark side of the moon.

Katy Moss Warner, general manager of Walt Disney World Parks Horticulture Division, not only eloquently addressed this problem, but pointed to a solution when she observed that "The future of the environment depends on involving children as early as possible in growing and appreciating plants, yet the worst-landscaped institutions in this country are the public schools."

Happily, that seems to be changing. All over the country, parents, teachers, and interested members of the community are going to PTAS and school administrations to request permission to install environmentally sound landscapes. And they're getting support from many resources, including local native-plant

San Dieguito High School, near San Diego, adopted a native landscape in 1990, thanks to the efforts of science teacher Jerry Trust. Even though Trust now teaches in another city, the work he began is carried on enthusiastically by students and teachers alike.

Songbirds on license plates is about as close as many people get to nature. But even that's too close for some. Back in the late eighties, a brave spirit in the Texas legislature proposed that the state's license plates be revised to include the words "The Wildflower State." Not unreasonable, considering all the work Lady Bird Johnson did promoting the brilliantly beautiful flora of her native state. But it was too much for the "bubbas" in the legislature, and the proposal was voted— make that hooted—down. Wildflowers didn't fit the super-macho Texan image they wanted to preserve.

societies, National Wildlife Federation's Schoolyard Habitat Program, the Audubon Society's School Sanctuary Program.

Clearly, the landscaping revolution involves taking a good hard look at what and how we are teaching our youngsters about nature. After all, they're the generation that's going to have to pull our environmental chestnuts out the fire. And the biggest lesson they need to know is that we do not live *apart* from nature . . . we *are* a part of nature.

Goose-Stepping Gooseberries and Other Myths

One of the ways you combat ignorance is with information. Facts. But when it comes to getting information on native plants and environmental landscaping, the reader faces something of a problem. During the past fifteen years or so, there's been a rash of negatively slanted articles on these subjects, ranging from merely misinformed to downright bizarre. Optimists within the landscaping revolution say that this backlash is proof that we're gaining in popularity.

Should We Call Her Miss Quotes?

A classic example of antinatural landscaping propaganda appeared in the August 21, 1998, edition of the prestigious *Wall Street Journal*. In "Where the Wild Things Are" by Rebecca Lowell, readers were told that having a natural landscape would place family

How Much Merit in These Badges?

Think about camping and hiking and communing with Mother Nature? You probably think of the Boy Scouts. Think about environmental education? Ditto. Unless, of course, you've perused some of their merit-badge manuals. In that case, you

might want to think again. The problem isn't only what they say, but often what they *don't* say!

Take the manual for the forestry merit badge. In it, you will read that clear-cutting—a practice virtually all conservation-

ists decry—is treated in a very, shall we say, tolerant manner. In fact, according to the Boy Scouts of America, clear-cutting can be beneficial. In the manual, it states that "clear-cutting actually creates habitat for many wildlife species that get part or all of their food, water, and shelter from low vegetation and brush with little or no overhead shade." Yeah, but what happens to the displaced wildlife that was there in the first place?

The manual conveniently ignores authorities such as Barry Flamm, chief forester for the Wilderness Society, who says that clear-cutting's impact "extends well beyond the area affected." Among other things, he says, clear-

What Boy Scouts learn in their forestry merit badge manual might surprise you!

In his *New York Times* article "Against Nativism" (May 15, 1994), Michael Pollan said that the natural garden movement has all but seized control in this country. Apparently this neighborhood didn't get the word.

cutting "pollutes streams, destroys valuable fisheries, and has a negative effect on biological diversity."

The Scouts' forestry manual also fails to mention that clear-cutting is just plain ugly—not unlike what strip mining does to the terrain. Pulitzer Prize–winning science writer William Dietrich wrote in his book *The Final Forest: The Battle for the Last Great Trees of the Pacific Northwest*, that clear-cutting is "a visible shock. The forest," he says, "looks not so much harvested as destroyed."

In the Boy Scout manual for the gardening merit badge, the scout is warned that pesticides "can be quite harmful to people and animals," and

he's given a list of precautions. That's good. But, he is *not* told a few facts that might dissuade him from resorting to chemical warfare in the first place. For instance, the scout is not told of the many scientific studies that link pesticides to a variety of maladies, ranging from skin rashes to birth defects to cancer.

Incredibly, the scout *is* told that a good way to dispose of pesticides is to "put them in a landfill dump." He is also told that he can combat plant mildew by using fungicides such as benomyl, which the EPA classifies as a possible human carcinogen (Class C), and actidione, which the EPA puts in Class One, its highest rating for acute toxicity.

David Chatfield, Director of Californians for Pesticide Reform (in his youth an Eagle Scout), says "these disposal methods are actually against the law in California. You can't even dispose of paint that way. Besides," he adds, "it's outrageous for the Boy Scouts of America to advise kids to use pesticides in the first place!"

Look, I'm not anti–Boy Scouts. I was a scout myself in the dim, dark past. My dad was an Eagle Scout and my father-in-law was a scoutmaster. I just wish the Boy Scouts of America would revise these manuals so that they don't sound like they'd been written by the public-relations people for the logging and chemical industries!

members in harm's way. And to back up her thesis, Lowell interviewed homeowners with "naturescapes" from around the country.

Anyone the least bit knowledgeable about the subject saw at once how biased and erroneous this article was. But most readers probably took it at face value, and ranked the idea of having a natural landscape just below tax audits on their lists of favorite things to do. When I first read the article I assumed that Lowell had found and quoted people who agreed with her premise. Imagine my surprise when I tracked down most of the people cited and got a very different slant on the story.

In the article, Coleen Kremer, of St. Petersburg, Florida, was quoted on the subject of black snakes, which, according to Lowell, lurk in the Kremers' tall grass and threaten life and limb. "The snakes sneak up

© Steve Breen, Copley News Service

Deer and other wildlife are found on many suburban landscapes—and very few of them could be called natural or naturalistic. Browsers and predators alike are forced to encroach into "civilization" because their natural habitats are disappearing. Coyotes have been seen on the grounds of a school in Colorado, and *Time* magazine reported that cougars were spotted near a shopping mall in Arizona.

on me, then I jump and scream," Coleen says in the article. "Nonsense," said her husband, Jeff, when we talked a few weeks later. "She was totally misquoted. Anyway, black snakes are very common around here—no matter what kind of landscape you have. They're harmless and nobody takes them seriously."

The Kremers were also, according to the article, responsible for their neighborhood being bombarded by yellow-crowned herons dropping "nasty bits of half-digested seafood" all over patios and lawn furniture. One neighbor, Debra Bittner, was quoted as putting the blame squarely on the Kremers' natural landscape for this "scourge of puke-balls."

In fact, Bittner told me that the tone of her comments was totally skewed. "The article made me sound angry. I wasn't and I'm not. It's not the Kremers' landscape that causes this, anyway. The herons live in the tall pines we have around here, and I told that reporter that I'd rather live with the puke-balls than not have the herons."

"The thing that really upset us," Jeff Kremer told me, "aside from misquoting us— is that this reporter had an agenda. She deliberately misrepresented to us what the story was going to be about. We thought she was writing a positive piece."

The word *agenda* popped up in a few other of my follow-up interviews. Greg Rubin, a San Diego landscape designer and the only professional cited by Lowell, was very outspoken about the article. "It was totally bogus and out of line," he said. "Rebecca Lowell admitted to me that she knew nothing about gardening, and it shows. She interviewed me and two of my clients at great length—over two hours each—and then picked a few comments out of context to make *her* point."

Joy Buslaff, an artist in Big Bend, Wisconsin, had a similar experience. The natural pond that she put in herself was presented as being a magnet for "thousands of toads." Joy told me that in fact there were

Sarah Squire, her daughter Beverly, and the "infamous" sandbox.

three toads. Later, she did have thousands of tadpoles, but "nature being what it is, almost all of them disappeared, eaten by other creatures. Frankly, I have more problems with neighbors' dogs than I do with wildlife," she stated.

The scariest part of Lowell's article for many was in reading that Colorado residents Mark and Sarah Squire had predatory coyotes in their children's sandbox, and black bears sitting in trees thanks to their natural landscape. The Squires' home, which is situated in the foothills of Cheyenne Mountain high above Colorado Springs, is in an area where such wildlife is often seen. The animals are a natural part of the environment, and are frequently spotted in the landscapes of other area residents, *even those with conventional lawn-centered landscapes*. Carrie Trookman reflected the comments of the other Squire neighbors I talked to about the wildlife situation. "We certainly don't live in

'If The Environmentalists Get Their Way, There Won't Be Any Trees Left To Cut'

fear of them," she said. "After all, we moved into their neighborhood, they didn't move into ours."

The tragedy is that many of these articles get reprinted all over the country, spreading the distortions and nonsense to people who, having no other information to rely on, assume, even in this day and age, that if it's in the media it's gotta be right.

It could be that the most serious consequence of our ignorance of nature is that environmentalism is not taken seriously. Public-opinion polls invariably place it near the bottom in lists of issues we care about. Environmentalists are labeled "eco-freaks," "tree-huggers," and "bleeding-heart wackos."

And when talk-show host Michael Reagan tells his listeners that "environmentalists care more about squirrels than they do about people," most of them nod in agreement.

The reason isn't hard to figure out: if what environmentalists are saying is true about the sorry state of our planet—even if it's only partially true—then that's scary! It's much easier to ridicule than to change. And ignorance can be very comforting. After all, what you don't know can't hurt you! Right?

Chapter 14

THE FAD THAT WON'T GO AWAY

What we found was that a grassroots movement (of natural landscapes) was quietly sweeping across the United States, one garden at a time.

Ken Druse
The Natural Habitat Garden

While giving a speech at the Dallas Arboretum in 1993, Peter Olin, director of the Minnesota Landscape Arboretum, dismissed the natural landscaping movement as a "craze." A fad!

Well, a fad, according to my dictionary, is "a temporary fashion." It is described as "a pursuit or interest followed usually widely but briefly and capriciously with exaggerated zeal." Fads are skinny trousers one year and bell-bottoms the next. Fads are hula hoops, mood rings, zoot suits, Nehru jackets, Tiny Tim, purple cars, Beanie Babies, and (one can only hope) blue nail polish. No way can anyone add the landscaping revolution to this list.

Interest and enthusiasm for native/natural landscaping has grown slowly but steadily . . .

The corporate world, too, is learning the advantages of going native. Aside from the natural beauty and environmental benefits, they are discovering savings in upkeep. This is the Sears National Headquarters outside Chicago.

gaining in popularity year by year, yet not overwhelming us in a paroxysm of ardor that would threaten to trivialize its very real value.

The Best Is Yet to Come

Where will the revolution be in ten or twenty years? According to Dr. David Northington, former executive director at the Lady Bird Johnson Wildflower Center, native landscapes will, by the second decade of the new century, be the norm. "The concept of using regional native wildflowers, grasses, shrubs, vines, and trees in our home and commercial landscapes will," he says, "have turned the corner. It will no longer be thought of as an interesting but esoteric notion, appealing only to a select audience."

If this strikes you as overly optimistic, consider this: if we had met sometime during the 1960s and I had told you that by the end of the twentieth century we'd be living in a society with nonsmoking rooms in hotels, nonsmoking airline flights, nonsmoking sections of restaurants, nonsmoking workplaces, no cigarette advertising in the media, and social gatherings where out of fifty or more guests only one was puffing away you'd have said I was nuts!

It took the better part of two hundred years for the lawn-centered landscape to achieve its dominant position in our society; yet it's becoming more and more evident that the native landscape will replace it in a fraction of that time. And it won't happen for aesthetic reasons alone, or because of lower maintenance requirements, or even because of the noble ideals of restoring wildlife habitats. It will happen for one inescapable and pragmatic reason. Water shortages will drive up the cost of this precious resource, making today's conventional landscapes not only impractical but, as Dr. Northington points out, "possibly even unpatriotic!"

A passing fad? As the late humorist Alexander King used to say, "Not a bit of it!"

The Lady Bird Johnson Wildflower Center

Mention the movie industry and you immediately think of Hollywood. Mention auto racing and you think of Indy or Daytona. Today, thanks to the efforts of a former first lady, Lady Bird Johnson, when anyone anywhere thinks about native plants, Austin, Texas, comes to mind.

The Lady Bird Johnson Wildflower Center was founded by Mrs. Johnson in 1982, and is dedicated to the preservation and reestablishment of America's indigenous flora. Located in the beautiful Hill Country southwest of Austin, the $9 million center is a model of environmentally correct construction techniques as well as water-conserving landscaping.

The new center—completed in 1995—was designed to be not merely functional, but aesthetically pleasing and environmentally sensitive. The intention was for it to blend harmoniously into the countryside, impacting its natural surroundings as little as possible. It was built using the envelope technique described in Chapter 11.

The Wildflower Center offers many colorful and fun attractions for the general public—a butterfly garden, children's garden, a water garden, a children's discovery room, and a forty-five-foot (14-m) stone observation tower. The architecture itself is worth the visit—dramatic and beautiful, with hints of old Spanish missions and limestone pioneer cabins. For most of the year, the landscape is a visual delight, vibrant with a wide palette of seasonal wildflowers. No wonder the center draws over one hundred thousand visitors per year.

As part of its charge to educate the public about native plants, the center has a modern

The forty-two-acre Lady Bird Johnson Wildflower Center in Austin contains demonstration gardens, a 232-seat auditorium for seminars, and educational facilities for young and old, professional and lay gardeners alike.

232-seat auditorium for conventions and seminars, attracting some of the leading native plant authorities from all over the world. There is also a special viewing room where a video, *Seeds for Tomorrow*, can be seen. In addition, the center conducts a two-week science and nature camp-out for young minority girls (Camp Wildflower), periodic teacher workshops, and guided tours of the gardens and grounds.

The center also operates as a national clearinghouse for native plant data, providing detailed guidelines and practical tips to gardeners from coast to coast. Its library contains a computer database of organizations, agencies, and individuals in all fifty states involved in native plant conservation, research, or landscaping, and its slide inventory has over fifteen thousand images of individual plants and landscapes, making it an

Landscaping Revolutionary Jim Hodgins

In the summer of 1984, eighty environmentally concerned native plant gardeners and field botanists met in Toronto, Canada, to form the Canadian Wildflower Society (now the North American Native Plant Society). At that meeting, it was decided that a magazine be created to integrate the interests and activities of both groups, and an editor be appointed. Jim Hodgins was the overwhelming choice.

The members knew Jim as a respected nature writer, wildflower gardener, and the author of *Flowers of the Wild: Ontario and the Great Lakes Region*. What they could not have known was just how much of himself Jim would, over the years, put into this publication—which was named

Wildflower. From issue number one until he retired from his teaching position at the University of Toronto in 1996, Jim held down *two* full-time jobs, the second being the editorship of this new publication. Moreover, for the first ten years of the magazine's life, Jim received not one cent in salary; it was truly a labor of love.

Under Jim's leadership, and with the help and encouragement of his wife, Zile Zichmanis, who serves as art and production manager, *Wildflower*

has grown from a simple black-and-white "cut-and-paste" effort into an attractive, modern, full-color publication that covers native botany not just in Canada but throughout North America, even down into the American Southwest.

Jim believes that a landscaping revolution is necessary to redress what he calls "the sickness of the land. We must learn to understand and work with the cycles and species in our own bioregions," he says. "In so doing, we heal both the land and ourselves."

Wildflower
Box 336, Postal Station F
Toronto, ON Canada
M4Y 2L7
E-mail: ann.melvin@
  sympatico.ca

invaluable resource for academics, professional landscapers, and lay gardeners alike. Fact sheets are available for small fees, identifying native species for each state, listing sources for seed and plants, and offering location-specific information on propagation and seed collection.

If a national native plant society should ever get off the ground—and many think it's inevitable—then they would certainly have the support and encouragement of the Lady Bird Johnson Wildflower Center. The current executive director, Robert Breunig, says, "I personally think it's going to happen, and we'd be happy to assist in its birth however we can." He points out that the Wildflower Center exists to aid and foster a national awareness of native plants, and to be "a positive partner to any organizations—national, regional, or statewide, that share our vision."

A Visit to the Old Neighborhood in 2035

A few years ago, I revisited Clifton, New Jersey, and the street where I'd grown up. I was surprised to see that this middle-class two-hundred-home subdivision had, if anything, improved. The homes had been well maintained over the years, and added onto—a backyard extension here and a dormer there—and the trees, little more than saplings back then, were now tall and full, giving the whole neighborhood a solid, established feel.

The lawns were still there, of course; the landscaping revolution had not yet reached Edison Street. Several sprinklers were anointing the turf grass as I drove by, and someone was running a power mower on the lawn in front of the old Donavan home.

I probably won't be around to see the old neighborhood in 2035, but I'll bet I can predict what it will look like. By then, if all estimates are on target, the lawns will be all gone, replaced by a variety of beautiful environmental landscapes. Bob and Ann Mullins' home will be graced by lush Christmas ferns, sweetferns, and bloodroot; the place where Ruth and John Miller once lived will sport a woodland flower garden beneath flowering dogwoods and mountain laurels; and the home I lived in will have a pocket prairie with big bluestem and New England aster gracing those slopes where I had once pushed that old rotary mower.

The sound of power equipment will have been forever banished, replaced by songbirds in greater abundance than ever. The odor of lawn chemicals will have long ago drifted away. And the current residents will be relaxing outdoors comfortably suspended in their zero-gravity lawn chairs, sipping icy cold syntho-colas, and watching the latest *Seinfeld* rerun on their 3-D, superhigh-definition combo sunglasses and video screens.

One of them—the neighborhood intellectual—will be doing an old-fashioned crossword puzzle on the laptop he's recently found in an antique shop. Stumped by one of the clues, he will call over to his next door neighbor. "Hey, Charlie, what's a nine-letter word for 'a device for cutting turf grass'?" Charlie will frown, deep in thought. After a moment or two, he will reply, "No idea."

Appendix

Native Plant Information Resources

Addresses and area codes subject to change

Alabama
Alabama Wildflower Society
240 Ivy Ln.
Auburn, AL 36830

Birmingham Botanical Gardens, The
2612 Lane Park Rd.
Birmingham, AL 35223
(205) 879-1227

Alaska
Alaska Native Plant Society
P.O. Box 141612
Anchorage, AK 99514-1613
(907) 333-8212
akkrafts@alaska.net

Georgeson Botanical Garden
University of Alaska Fairbanks
West Tanana Dr.
P.O. Box 757200
Fairbanks, AK 99775-7200
(907) 474-5651

Arizona
Arizona Native Plant Society
P.O. Box 41206
Sun Station
Tuscon, AZ 85717
anps@azstarnet.com

Arizona-Sonora Desert Museum
2021 N. Kinney Rd.
Tuscon, AZ 85743
(520) 883-2702

Mountain States Wholesale Nursery
10020 West Glendale Ave.
Glendale, AZ 85307
(602) 247-8509

Arkansas
Arkansas Arboretum
Pinnacle Mountain State Park
11901 Pinnacle Valley Rd.
Roland, AR 72135
(501) 868-5806

Arkansas Native Plant Society
Department of Math and Sciences
University of Arkansas
Monticello, AR 71655
(870) 460-1165 or (870) 460-1066
sundell@uamont.edu

California
California Native Plant Society
1722 J Street, Suite 17
Sacramento CA 95814
(707) 882-1655
www.cnps.org

Living Desert, The
47900 South Portola Ave.
Palm Desert, CA 92260
(760) 346-5690

Rancho Santa Ana Botanic Garden
1500 North College Ave.
Claremont, CA 91711
(909) 625-8767

Santa Barbara Botanic Garden
1212 Mission Canyon Rd.
Santa Barbara, CA 93105
(805) 682-4726

Society for Pacific Coast Native Iris
977 Meredith Ct.
Sonomia, CA 95476

Southern California Botanists
Department of Biology
Fullerton State University
Fullerton, CA 92634
(714) 278-7034
aromspert@fullerton.edu

Theodore Payne Foundation
10549 Tuxford St.
Sun Valley, CA 91352
(818) 768-1802
theodorepayne@juno.com

Colorado
Colorado Native Plant Society
P.O. Box 200
Fort Collins, CO 80522

District of Columbia
Kenilworth Aquatic Gardens
1900 Anacostia Ave. NE
Washington, D.C. 20020
(202) 426-6905

Florida
Florida Native Plant Society
P.O. Box 6116
Spring Hill, FL 34611-6116
(352) 856-8202

Georgia
Atlanta Botanical Garden
1345 Piedmont Ave.
Atlanta, GA 30309
(404) 876-5859

Georgia Native Plant Society
P.O. Box 422085
Atlanta, GA 30342
(770) 343-6000
HDeV@juno.com

Hawaii
National Tropical Botanical Garden
P.O. Box 340
Lawai, Kauai, HI 96765
(808) 332-7324

Idaho
Idaho Botanical Garden
2355 N. Penitentiary Rd.
Boise, ID 83712
(208) 343-8649

Idaho Native Plant Society
P.O. Box 9451
Boise, ID 83707
www2.state.id.us/fishgame/
   inps.htm

Illinois
Grand Prairie Friends
www.prairienet.org

Illinois Native Plant Society
20301 E. 900 N Rd.
Westville, IL 61883
(217) 662-2142
ilnps@aol.com

Lincoln Memorial Garden and Nature
Center
2301 East Lake Dr.
Springfield, IL 62707
(217) 529-1111

Southern Illinois Native Plant Society
Botany Department
Southern Illinois University
Carbondale, IL 52901

Indiana

Hayes Regional Arboretum
801 Elks Rd.
Richmond, IN 47374-2526
(765) 962-3745

Indiana Native Plant & Wildflower
Society
5952 Lieber Rd.
Indianapolis, IN 46228-1319
(812) 988-0063
pharstad@topaz.iupui.edu

Iowa

Des Moines Botanical Center
909 East River Dr.
Des Moines, IA 50316
(515) 242-2934

Iowa Prairie Network
P.O. Box 516
Mason City, IA 50402-0516
www.netins.net/showcase/
    bluestem/ipnapp.htm

Kansas

Cimarron National Grassland
242 East Hwy. 56
Elkhart, KS 67950
(316) 697-4621

Kansas Wildflower Society
R. L. McGregor Herbarium
2045 Constant Ave.
Lawrence, KS 66047-3729
(785) 864-5093
c-freeman@ukans.edu

Kentucky

Kentucky Native Plant Society
Department of Biological Studies
East Kentucky University
Richmond, KY 40475
(606) 622-2258
http://157.89.1.144/bio/jones/
    knps.htm

Land Between the Lakes
Tennessee Valley Authority
100 Van Morgan Rd.
Golden Pond, KY 42211

Louisiana

Lafayette Natural History Museum
637 Girard Park Dr.
Lafayette, LA 70504
(318) 291-5581

Louisiana Native Plant Society
R.R. 1, Box 151
Saline, LA 71070

Society for Louisiana Irises
1812 Broussard Rd. E.
Lafayette, LA 70508
(318) 856-5859

Maine

Wild Gardens of Acadia
Acadia National Park
P.O. Box 177
Bar Harbor, ME 04609
(207) 288-3338

Maryland

Chesapeake Audubon Society
Rare Plant Committee
P.O. Box 3173
Baltimore, MD 21228

Maryland Native Plant Society
14720 Claude Ln.
Silver Spring, MD 20904

Massachusetts

Conway School of Landscape Design,
The
46 Delabarre Ave.
Conway, MA 01341-0179
(413) 369-4044
info@csld.edu

New England Wild Flower Society
180 Hemenway Rd.
Framingham, MA 01701-2699
(508) 877-7630
www.newfs.org

Michigan

Fernwood Botanic Garden
13988 Range Line Rd.
Niles, MI 49120
(616) 695-6491

Wildflower Association of Michigan
3853 Farrell Rd.
Hastings, MI 49058
(616) 948-2496
marjif@iserv.net

Minnesota

Minnesota Landscape Arboretum
University of Minnesota
3675 Arboretum Dr.
Chanhassen, MN 55317-0039
(612) 443-2460

Minnesota Native Plant Society
220 Biological Science Center
University of Minnesota
1445 Gortner Ave.
St. Paul, MN 55108
(651) 773-9207
mnps@altavista.net
www.stolaf.edu/depts/biology/
    mnps

Mississippi

Mississippi Native Plant Society
111 North Jefferson St.
Jackson, MS 39201
(601) 354-7303

Missouri

Center for Plant Conservation
Missouri Botanical Garden
P.O. Box 299
St. Louis, MO 63166-0299
(314) 577-9450

Missouri Native Plant Society
P.O. Box 20073
St. Louis, MO 63144-0073

Missouri Prairie Foundation, The
Box 200
Columbia, MO 65205
www.moprairie.org

Shaw Arboretum
P.O. Box 38
Gray Summit, MO 63039
(314) 577-5142

Montana

Montana Native Plant Society
P.O. Box 992
Bozeman, MT 59771

Montana State University Arboretum
W. College Ave. and S. 11th Ave.
Bozeman, MT 59717
(406) 994-5048

Nebraska

Homestead National Monument
Route 3, Box 47
Beatrice, NE 68310
(402) 223-3514

Prairie/Plains Resource Institute
1307 L St.
Aurora, NE 68818
(402) 694-5535
ppri@hamilton.net

Nevada

Desert Demonstration Garden
3701 W. Alta Dr.
Las Vegas, NV 89153
(702) 258-3205

Mojave Native Plant Society
8180 Placid Dr.
Las Vegas, NV 89123

Northern Nevada Native Plant
Society
P.O. Box 8965
Reno, NV 89507-8965

New Jersey

New Jersey Native Plant Society
Cook College, Office of Continuing
Education
P.O. Box 231
New Brunswick, NJ 08903-0231

Tourne County Park
53 E. Hanover Ave.
Morristown, NJ 07962-1295
(973) 326-7600

New Mexico

Living Desert Zoo and Gardens
1504 Miehls Dr.
Carlsbad, NM 88220
(505) 887-5516

Native Plant Society of New Mexico
P.O. Box 5917
Santa Fe, NM 87502-5917
(505) 454-0683
whitmore@nmha.campuscw.net
www.wazoo.com/~dkeeney/
    npsoc.html

New York

Brooklyn Botanic Garden
1000 Washington Ave.
Brooklyn, NY 11225
lorigold@bbg.org
www.bbg.org
(718) 398-2400

Cooperative Sanctuary Program
Audubon International
46 Rarick Rd.
Selkirk, NY 12158
(518) 767-9051

North Carolina

North Carolina Native Plant Society
900 West Nash St.
Wilson, NC 27893

North Dakota

Gunlogson Nature Preserve
Icelandic State Park
13571 Hwy. 5 West
Cavalier, ND 58220
(701) 265-4561

Ohio

Ohio Native Plant Society
6 Louise Dr.
Chagrin Falls, OH 44022

Wegerzyn Horticultural Association
1301 E. Siebenthaler Ave.
Dayton, OH 45414
(937) 277-9028
www.dayton.net/MetroParks

Oklahoma

Oklahoma Native Plant Society
2435 Peoria Ave.
Tulsa, OK 74114

Oxley Nature Center
6700 E. Mohawk Blvd.
Tulsa, OK 74115
(918) 669-6644

Oregon

Native Plant Society of Oregon
2584 NW Savier St.
Portland, OR 97210
(503) 248-9242
www.teleport.com/nonprofit/
    npso/

Natural Areas Association
P.O. Box 1504
Bend, OR 97709
(541) 317-0199
naa@natareas.org

Pennsylvania

Bowman's Hill Wildflower Preserve
Route 32, River Rd.
New Hope, PA 18938
(215) 862-2924

Brandywine Conservancy Wildflower
and Native Plant Gardens
Route 1
Chadds Ford, PA 19317
(610) 388-2700

Shenk's Ferry Wildflower Preserve
9 New Village Rd.
Holtwood, PA 17532
(717) 284-2278

Rhode Island

Rhode Island Native Plant Society
P.O. Box 114
Peace Dale, RI 02883

South Carolina

South Carolina Native Plant Society
P.O. Box 759
Pickens, SC 29671
(864) 878-1786
tgoforth@innova.net
www.scnativeplants.org

Wildflower Alliance of South Carolina
P.O. Box 12181
Columbia, SC 29211
(803) 799-6889

South Dakota

Great Plains Native Plant Society
P.O. Box 461
Hot Springs, SD 57747
(605) 745-3397
cascade@gwtc.net

Tennessee

Tennessee Native Plant Society
227 E. Brushy Valley
Powell, TN 37849

Texas

Chihuahuan Desert Research
Institute
P.O. Box 1334
Alpine, TX 79831

El Paso Native Plant Society
7760 Maya Ave.
El Paso, TX 79931

Native Plant Society of Texas
P.O. Box 891
Georgetown, TX 78627
(512) 238-0695
www.lonestar.texas.net/
    ~jleblanc/npsot.html

Native Prairies Association of Texas
3503 Lafayette Ave.
Austin, TX 78722-1807
(512)480-3059
www.sunsetc.com/npat/index.
    html

Utah

Natural Resources Conservation
Service
125 South State St., Rm. 4402
Salt Lake City, UT 84138

Utah Native Plant Society
3631 South Carolyn St.
Salt Lake City, UT 84106

Virginia

Eastern Native Plant Alliance
P.O. Box 6101
McLean, VA 22106

Virginia Native Plant Society
P.O. Box 844
Annandale, VA 22033

Washington

NatureScaping Wildlife Botanical
Gardens
11000 N.E. 149th St.
Vancouver, WA 98682
(360) 604-4400

Washington Native Plant Society
P.O. Box 28690
Seattle, WA 98118-8690
(888) 288-8022
wnps@blarg.net
www.televar.com~donew/
    wwnps.html

West Virginia

West Virginia Native Plant Society
P.O. Box 2755
Elkins, WV 26241

Wisconsin

Society for Ecological Restoration
University of Wisconsin Arboretum
1207 Seminole Hwy.
Madison, WI 53711
(608) 262-9547

Wehr Nature Center
9701 W. College Ave.
Franklin, WI 53132
(414) 425-8550

Wyoming

Wyoming Native Plant Society
P.O. Box 1471
Cheyenne, WY 82003

National

Center for Plant Conservation
P.O. Box 229
St. Louis, MO 63166
http://cisus.mobot.org/CPC

Lady Bird Johnson Wildflower Center,
The
4801 LaCrosse Ave.
Austin, TX 78739
(512) 292-4200
www.wildflower.org

Native Plant Conservation Initiative
1849 C St., NW, LSB 204
Washington, D.C. 20240
(202) 452-0392
www.nps.gov/plants/coop.htm

National Wildlife Federation
8925 Leesburg Pike
Vienna, VA 22184-0001
(800) 822-9919
www.nwf.org

Nature Conservancy, The
1815 North Lynn St.
Arlington, VA 22209
(703) 841-5300
www.tnc.org

Wild Ones—Natural Landscapers, Ltd.
P.O. Box 23576
Milwaukee, WI 23576
(312) 845-5116
www.for-wild.org

Wildlands Project, The
1955 West Grant Rd., Ste. 148
Tucson, AZ 85745
(520) 884-0875

Canada

Canadian Nature Federation
1 Nicholas St., Ste. 606
Ottawa, ON K1N 7B7
(800) 267-4088 or (613) 562-3447
www.cnf.ca

Canadian Wildlife Federation
2740 Queensview Dr.
Ottawa, ON K2B 1A2
(613) 721-2286

Evergreen Foundation, The
355 Adelaide St. West, #5A
Toronto, ON M5V 1S2
(604) 689-0766
info@evergreen.ca

Native Plant Society of British
Columbia, The
2012 William St.
Vancouver, BC V5L 2X6
(604) 255-5719

North American Native Plant
Society
P.O. Box 336, Station F
Toronto, ON M4Y 2L7

BIBLIOGRAPHY

Ajilvsgi, Geyata. *Butterfly Gardening for the South*. Dallas: Taylor Publishing, 1990.

Asimov, Isaac, and Frederick Pohl. *Our Angry Earth*. New York: Tor Books, 1991.

Bailey, L. H. *Manual of Cultivated Plants*. New York: Macmillan, 1949.

Bassett, Karen. "The Red List of Threatened Plants." *Native Plants*, 16, no.2 (Spring 1999).

Begley, Sharon. "Aliens Invade America!" *Newsweek*, August 10, 1998.

Bormann, F. Herbert, Diana Balmori, and Gordon T. Geballe. *Redesigning the American Lawn: A Search for Environmental Harmony*. New Haven, Conn.: Yale University Press, 1993.

Breunig, Robert. "Our Work Has Never Been More Important." *Native Plants*, 16, no.1 (Winter 1999).

Brooklyn Botanic Garden. *The Natural Lawn & Alternatives*. Edited by Janet Marinelli. New York: Author, 1993.

——*Going Native: Biodiversity in Our Own Backyards*. Edited by Janet Marinelli. New York: Author, 1994.

Browning, Michael. "As Supplies Dwindle and Populations Grow." *Miami Herald*, May 27, 1998.

Buchmann, Stephen L., and Gary Paul Nabhan. *The Forgotten Pollinators*. Washington D.C.: Island Press, 1996.

Clarke, Gilliam. "Desalination Wave of Our Future for Water Needs." *St. Petersburg Times*, May 25, 1998.

Cundiff, Bred. "Lands for Life." *Wildflower* (summer 1998).

Daniels, Stevie. *The Wild Lawn Handbook*. New York: Macmillan, 1995.

Denver Water Department. *Xeriscape Plant Guide*. Golden, Colo.: Fulcrum Publishing, 1996.

Durnil, Gordon K. *The Making of a Conservative Environmentalist*. Bloomington: Indiana University Press, 1995.

Fantle, Will. "Why Johnny Can't Breed." *Isthmus, the Weekly Newspaper of Madison*, August 5, 1994.

Fisher, Kathleen. "Class Act." *The American Gardener*, January–February, 1998.

Gallup, Barbara, and Deborah Reich. *The Complete Book of Topiary*. New York: Workman Publishing, 1987.

Graves, William, ed. *Water: The Power, Promise and Turmoil of North America's Fresh Water*, Washington, D.C.: National Geographic, 1993.

Green, Nick. "Hike in Water Rates on Tap." *Los Angeles Times*, May 20, 1988.

Haukos, David A., and Loren M. Smith. *Common Flora of the Playa Lakes*, Lubbock: Texas Tech University Press, 1997.

Hiaasen, Carl. *Team Rodent: How Disney Devours the World*. New York: The Ballantine Publishing Group, 1998.

Hollingsworth, Craig, and Karen Idoine. "An Environmental Gardener's Guide to Pest Management." In *The Environmental Gardener*. Handbook 130. Brooklyn: Brooklyn Botanic Garden, spring 1992.

Jenkins, Virginia Scott. *The Lawn: A History of an American Obsession*. Washington, D.C.: Smithsonian Institution Press, 1994.

Knopf, Jim, Sally Wasowski, John Kadel Boring, Glenn Keator, Jane Scott, and Erica Glasener. *Natural Gardening*. Berkeley, Calif.: The Nature Company, 1995.

Metcalf, C. L., and W. P. Flint. *Destructive and Useful Insects*. New York: McGraw-Hill, 1928.

Orr, Oliver H., Jr. *Saving American Birds*. Gainesville: University Press of Florida, 1992.

Randall, John M., and Janet Marinelli. *Invasive Plants: Weeds of the Global Garden*. Brooklyn: Brooklyn Botanic Garden, 1996.

Robinson, Scott K. "The Case of the Missing Songbirds." *Consequences* 3, no. 1 (1997).

Royal Horticultural Society, The. *The Wisley Book of Gardening*. Edited by Robert Pearson. Feltham, England: Author, 1981.

Sauer, Leslie Jones. *The Once and Future Forest: A Guide to Forest Restoration Strategies*. Washington D.C.: Island Press, 1998.

Schneck, Marcus. *Butterflies: How to Identify and Attract Them to Your Garden*. Emmaus, Pa.: Rodale Press, 1990.

Sharp, Curtis W., George A. White, and James A. Briggs. "The Plants That Followed People." In *Our American Land: 1987 Yearbook of Agriculture*. Washington, D.C.: USDA, 1987.

Steger, Will, and Jon Bowermaster. *Saving the Earth*. New York: Alfred A. Knopf, 1991.

Taylor, M., and C. Hill. *Hardy Plants Introduced to Britain by 1799*, 2nd ed. Hatfield, England: Hatfield House, 1972.

Time-Life Books. *Pests & Diseases*. Complete Gardener Series. Alexandria, Va.: Time-Life, 1995.

Vanden Brook, Tom. "School's Prairie Garden Destroyed by Blacktop." *Milwaukee Journal Sentinel*, September 7, 1998.

Wasowski, Sally, and Andy Wasowski. *Requiem for a Lawnmower*. Dallas: Taylor Publishing, 1992.

——*Gardening with Native Plants of the South*. Dallas: Taylor Publishing, 1994.

——*Native Gardens for Dry Climates*. New York: Clarkson-Potter, 1995.

——*Native Texas Plants: Landscaping Region, by Region*. 2nd ed. Houston: Gulf Publishing, 1997.

"Water Challenges." editorial, *Jerusalem Post*, June 3, 1998.

Winslow, Susan, producer. *The Power of Water*: National Geographic television special, November 10, 1993.

INDEX

Page numbers in *italic* refer to illustrations.